TEXTBOOK OF

First Steps into Cloud Computing

(FIRST EDITION)

Dr. Tejinder Kaur (1st Author)
(Associate Professor)
DEPARTMENT OF MMICTBM
MMEC, MMDU, Mullana,
Ambala, Haryana (133207)

Dr. Vivek Bhatnagar (2nd Co-Author)
(Professor)
DEPARTMENT OF MMICTBM
MMEC, MMDU, Mullana,
Ambala, Haryana (133207)

Dr. Ankita (3rd Author)
(Assistant Professor)
Department of Computer Applications,
Panipat Institute of Engineering and
Technology, Samalkha, Haryana
(132102)

Dr. Anima Bag (4th Author)
(Assistant Professor)
Department of Statistics Rama Devi Women's
University, Bhubaneswar, Odisha
(751022)

Expert Notes, Publisher
Karnal (Haryana)-132001
Visit Us at www.expertnotes.in.

First Steps into Cloud Computing

Karnal (Haryana)-132001

www.expertnotes.in.

Book design by Expert Notes, Publisher

www.expertnotes.in.

ISBN: - 978-93-49922-19-8 (E-Book)

ISBN: - 978-93-49922-19-8 (E-Book)

Book design by Cover Designer

www.expertnotes.in

Published by Expert Notes, Publisher

Karnal (Haryana)-132001

www.expertnotes.in

Perface by Dr.Tejinder Kaur

Dr. Tejinder Kaur is a distinguished Associate Professor in the Department of MMICTBM at Maharishi Markandeshwar Engineering College (MMEC), a part of the esteemed Maharishi Markandeshwar (Deemed to be University), Mullana, Ambala, Haryana. With an extensive academic background and a strong dedication to research and teaching, Dr. Kaur has made remarkable contributions to the field of Computer engineering.

Throughout her career, Dr. Kaur has actively engaged in high-impact research, publishing papers in SCI and Scopus-indexed journals, and presenting her work at international conferences. DR.Kaur has published papers in Q2 journal. Dr.Kaur's patents are 60+. Book is also published on Computer Architecture, from idea to impact :a student's guide to entrepreneurship,cyber security : a comprehensive perspective, intellectual property rights unlocked: your rights,your power.

Guided 4 students of PHD, Guided 3 international students in M.TECH. Beyond research, Dr. Kaur is deeply involved in academic administration, skilfully managing various responsibilities while also fostering a dynamic learning environment for students. She has been instrumental in organizing student events, industrial visits, and technical workshops, thereby bridging the gap between theoretical knowledge and practical applications.

Wishing you an informed, empowered, and impactful journey ahead.

Dr. Tejinder Kaur

(Author & Associate Professor in the Department of MMICTBM at Maharishi Markandeshwar Institutes of Computer Technology & Business Management, Mullana)

Perface by Dr. Vivek Bhatnagar

Dr. Vivek Bhatnagar, Professor & Head of Department MMICT&BM (MCA), Maharishi Markandeshwar (Deemed to be University) Dr. Vivek Bhatnagar has been an integral Part of Maharishi Markandeshwar (Deemed to be University) since June 2004, bringing over 22 years of teaching experience. Throughout his academic career, Dr. Bhatnagar has been actively engaged in national and international seminars and has made significant contributions to research and innovation. He has authored over 35 research papers in prestigious international journals, including SCI and Scopus-indexed publications, as well as Springer journals. Furthermore, he holds five patents registered with the Intellectual Property India and has secured three copyrights. An advocate for lifelong learning, Dr. Bhatnagar has attended various short-term courses and workshops, expanding his knowledge and expertise. His contributions to academia include the authorship of three books: Textbook of Computers, Internet Service, Challenges, and Applications, Software Development Life Cycle at a Glance (available as an e-book on Amazon) In addition to his research and teaching, he has guided MPhil students and is currently mentoring three PhD candidates. As a certified Publon reviewer, he has assessed numerous research papers for leading international journals. Dr. Bhatnagar is deeply involved in student development, having organized various technical events, industrial visits, workshops, and job fests aimed at enhancing learning experiences. His international exposure includes visits to the USA, Germany, France, the Netherlands, Belgium, Dubai, Malaysia, Thailand, and Bali, where he has collaborated with professors to explore performance testing tools and software project management. During his most recent visit to the USA in January 2025, Dr. Bhatnagar engaged with faculty at California State University, Irvine State University, and San Diego State University, exchanging insights on project-based learning methodologies. He also visited ADP, a leading payroll and IT solutions company, where he had meaningful discussions with Mr. Manish, Senior Vice President of Product Development & Operations, about cutting-edge tools utilizing generative AI. Beyond academia, Dr. Bhatnagar plays a pivotal role in academic administration, student engagement, and media-related activities at the university, serving as a sessional coordinator and contributing to institutional growth.

Dr. Vivek Bhatnagar, (Professor & Head of Department MMICT&BM (MCA), Maharishi Markandeshwar (Deemed to be University)

Perface by Dr. Ankita

Dr. Ankita is an Assistant Professor in the department of Computer Applications at Panipat Institute of Engineering and Technology, Samalkha (an autonomous institute). She has a strong dedication to research. Her research interests are Artificial intelligence, machine learning, and wireless networking. She has published various research papers in national and international conferences and also published papers in SCI and Scopus. She also owns multiple patents in her name. She focuses more on practical knowledge than theoretical knowledge and makes the best use of knowledge.

Dr. Ankita

Assistant Professor in the department of Computer Applications at Panipat Institute of Engineering and Technology, Samalkha

Perface by Dr. Anima Bag

Dr. Anima Bag currently serves as the Assistant Professor and Head of the Department of Statistics at Rama Devi Women's University (RDWU), Odisha. She earned her Postgraduate, M.Phil., and Ph.D. degrees from Utkal University, Bhubaneswar, Odisha, India. In addition to her academic roles, she is the Nodal Officer of the Census Data Research Workstation at RDWU.Dr. Bag has been actively engaged in academic administration, efficiently handling multiple responsibilities. She has represented the Department of Statistics at the national level by facilitating student participation in the annual training programmes organized by the National Statistical Systems Training Academy (NSSTA), Greater Noida, Uttar Pradesh. She also played a key role in designing the postgraduate syllabus for the Department of Statistics at RDWU. With 14 years of teaching experience and 12 years in research, her areas of expertise include Operations Research, Inventory Control, Supply Chain Management, Multivariate Analysis, Optimization Techniques, Demography, and Machine Learning. She has also organized and conducted numerous seminars and workshops to enhance academic engagement. Dr. Bag has been recognized with several national and international awards for her academic achievements. Most notably, she received the Lifetime Achievement Award from the Vargava Foundation for Research and Education, Jharkhand, an organization registered under the Ministry of MSME, Government of India.

She is a life member of the Indian Society for Probability and Statistics (ISPS) and the International Journal for Research Under Literal Access (IJRULA). Her scholarly contributions include numerous publications in reputed national and international journals, presentations at various seminars and conferences, peer reviews of research articles, and authorship of book chapters. Dr. Bag has also successfully mentored 24 student research projects.

Dr. Anima Bag

Assistant Professor and Head of the Department of Statistics at Rama Devi Women's University (RDWU), Odisha

INDEX

UNIT -1

Scalable Computing over the Internet

High-Throughput Computing-HTC

HTC paradigm pays more attention to high-flux computing. The main application for high-flux computing is in Internet searches and web services by millions or more users simultaneously. The performance measures high throughput or the number of tasks completed per unit of time. HTC technology needs to improve batch processing speed, and also address the acute problems of cost, energy savings, security, and reliability at many data and enterprise computing centers

Computing Paradigm Distinctions

- **Centralized computing**
  - This is a computing paradigm by which all computer resources are centralized in one physical system.
  - All resources (processors, memory, and storage) are fully shared and tightly coupled within one integrated OS.
  - Many data centers and supercomputers are centralized systems, but they are used in parallel, distributed, and cloud computing applications.

• **Parallel computing**

- In parallel computing, all processors are either tightly coupled with centralized shared memory or loosely coupled with distributed memory
- . Interprocessor communication is accomplished through shared memory or via message passing.
- A computer system capable of parallel computing is commonly known as a parallel computer
- Programs running in a parallel computer are called parallel programs. The process of writing parallel programs is often referred to as parallel programming

• **Distributed computing**

- A distributed system consists of multiple autonomous computers, each having its own private memory, communicating through a computer network.

- Information exchange in a distributed system is accomplished through message passing.
- A computer program that runs in a distributed system is known as a distributed program.
- The process of writing distributed programs is referred to as distributed programming.
- Distributed computing system uses multiple computers to solve large-scale problems over the Internet using a centralized computer to solve computational problems.

• **Cloud computing**

- An Internet cloud of resources can be either a centralized or a distributed computing system. The cloud applies parallel or distributed computing, or both.
- Clouds can be built with physical or virtualized resources over large data centers that are centralized or distributed.
- Cloud computing can also be a form of utility computing or service computing

Degrees of Parallelism

- **Bit-level parallelism** (BLP) :
    - converts bit-serial processing toword-level processing gradually.
- **Instruction-levelparallelism** (ILP)
    - the processor executes multiple instructions simultaneously rather thanonly one instruction at a time.
    - ILP is executed through pipelining, superscalarcomputing, VLIW (very long instruction word) architectures, and multithreading.
    - ILP requiresbranch prediction, dynamic scheduling, speculation, and compiler support to work efficiently.
- **Data-level parallelism** (DLP)
    - DLP through SIMD (single instruction, multipledata) and vector machines using vector or array types of instructions.
    - DLP requires even more hardwaresupport and compiler assistance to work properly.
- **Task-level parallelism (TLP):**
    - Ever since the introduction of multicoreprocessors and chip multiprocessors (CMPs), we have been exploring TLP
    - TLP is far from beingvery successful due to difficulty in programming and compilation of

code for efficient execution onmulticore CMPs.

- **Utility Computing**
  - Utility computing focuses on a business model in which customers receive computing resources from a paid service provider. All grid/cloud platforms are regarded as utility service providers.

- **The Internet of Things (IoT)**
  - Traditional Internet connects machines to machines or web pages to web pages.
  - IoT was introduced in 1999 at MIT
  - networked interconnection of everyday objects, tools, devices, or computers
  - a wireless network of sensors that interconnect all things in our daily life.
  - Three communication patterns co-exist: namely H2H (human-to-human), H2T (human-tothing),and T2T (thing-to-thing).
  - connect things (including human and machine objects) at any time and any place intelligently with low cost
  - IPv6 protocol, 2128 IP addresses are available to distinguish all the objects on Earth, including all computers and pervasive devices
  - IoT needs to be designed to track 100 trillion static or moving objects simultaneously.
  - IoT demands universal addressability of all of the objects orthings.
  - The dynamic connections will grow exponentially into a new dynamic network ofnetworks, called the Internet of Things (IoT).

Cyber-Physical Systems

- A cyber-physical system (CPS) is the result of interaction between computational processes and the physical world.
- CPS integrates "cyber" (heterogeneous, asynchronous) with "physical" (concurrent and information-dense) objects

- CPS merges the "3C" technologies of computation, communication, and control into an intelligent closed feedback system

IoT emphasizes various networking connections among physical objects, while the CPS emphasiz exploration of virtual reality (VR) applications in the physical world

TECHNOLOGIES FOR NETWORK-BASED SYSTEMS

Multicore CPUs and Multithreading Technologies: Today, advanced CPUs or microprocessor chi assume a multicore architecture with dual, quad, six, or more processing cores. These processors explo parallelism at ILP and TLP levels. Both multi-core CPU and many-core GPU processors can handle multip instruction threads at different magnitudes today. Multiple cores are housed in the same chip with an L2 cach that is shared by all cores. In the future, multiple CMPs could be built on the same CPU chip with even the L cache on the chip. Multicore and multithreaded CPUs are equipped with many high-end processors, includin the Intel i7, Xeon, AMD Opteron, Sun Niagara, IBM Power 6, and X cell processors. Each core could be als multithreaded.

Memory, Storage, and Wide-Area Networking: Memory chips have experienced a 4x increase in capacit every three years. For hard drives, capacity increased from 260 MB in 1981 to 250 GB in 2004. Disks or dis arrays have exceeded 3 TB in capacity. The rapid growth of flash memory and solid-state drives (SSDs) als impacts the future of HPC and HTC systems.

System-Area Interconnects: The nodes in small clusters are mostly interconnected by an Ethernet switch o a local area network(LAN).

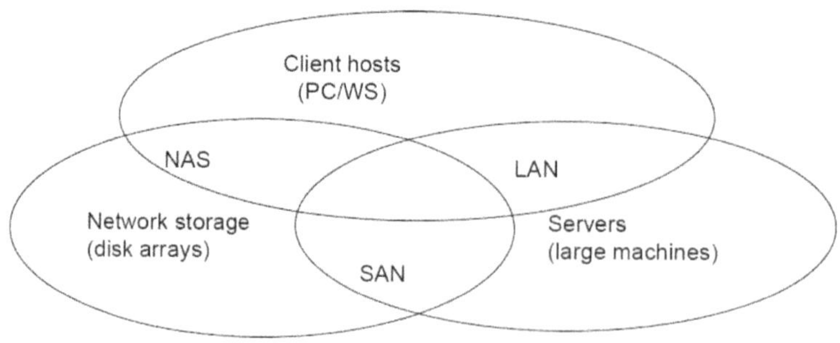

As Figure shows, a LAN typically is used to connect client hosts to big servers.A storage area network (SAN connects servers to network storage such as disk arrays. Network attached storage (NAS) connects client host

directly to the disk arrays. All three types of networks often appear in a large cluster built with commercial network components.

Wide-Area Networking: High-bandwidth networking increases the capability of building massively distributed systems. The rapid growth of Ethernet bandwidth from 10 Mbps in1979 to 1 Gbps in 1999, and 40 ~ 100 GE in 2011. It has been speculated that 1 Tbps network links will become available by 2013.

Virtual Machines and Virtualization Middleware

Virtual machines (VMs) offer novel solutions to underutilized resources, application inflexibility, software manageability, and security concerns in existing physical machines. Today, to build large clusters, grids, and clouds, we need to access large amounts of computing, storage, and networking resources in a virtualized manner. We need to aggregate those resources, and hopefully, offer a single system image. In particular, a cloud of provisioned resources must rely on virtualization of processors, memory, and I/O facilities dynamically.

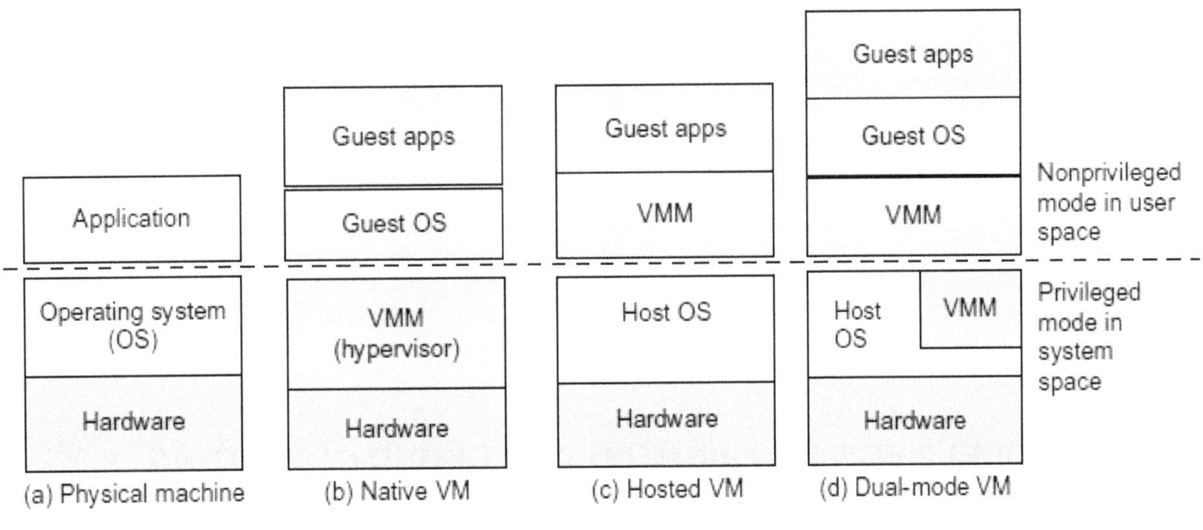

Three VM architectures in (b), (c), and (d), compared with the traditional physical machine shown in (a).

The host machine is equipped with the physical hardware. The VM is built with virtual resources managed by a guest OS to run a specific application. Between the VMs and the host platform, one needs to deploy a middleware layer called a virtual machine monitor (VMM).

Figure shows a native VM installed with the use of a VMM called a hypervisor in privileged Mode. The guest OS could be a Linux system and the hypervisor is the XEN system developed at Cambridge University. This hypervisor approach is also called bare-metal VM, because the hyperviso handles the bare hardware (CPU, memory, and I/O) directly. Architecture is the host VM shown in Figure(c) Here the VMM runs in non-privileged mode. The host OS need not be modified. The VM can also b implemented with a dual mode, as shown in Figure 1.12(d). Part of the VMM runs at the user level an another part runs at the supervisor level. In this case, the host OS may have to be modified to some extent Multiple VMs can be ported to a given hardware system to support the virtualization process. The VM approach offers hardware independence of the OS and applications.

VM Primitive Operations: The VMM provides the VM abstraction to the guest OS. With full virtualization the VMM exports a VM abstraction identical to the physical machine so that a standard OS such as Window 2000 or Linux can run just as it would on the physical hardware

Low-level VMM operations are

- the VMs can be multiplexed between hardware machines,
- a VM can be suspended and stored in stable storage
- a suspended VM can be resumed or provisioned to a new hardware platform
- a VM can be migrated from one hardware platform to another

These VM operations enable a VM to be provisioned to any available hardware platform. They also enable flexibility in porting distributed application executions. Furthermore, the VM approach will significantly enhance the utilization of server resources.

SYSTEM MODELS FOR DISTRIBUTED AND CLOUD COMPUTING

- Distributed and cloud computing systems are built over a large number of autonomous computer nodes. These node machines are interconnected by SANs, LANs, or WANs
- A massive system is with millions of computers connected to edge networks.
- Massive systems are considered highly scalable

- massive systems are classified into four groups: clusters, P2P networks, computing grids, and Internet clouds

Table 1.2 Classification of Parallel and Distributed Computing Systems

Functionality, Applications	Computer Clusters [10,28,38]	Peer-to-Peer Networks [34,46]	Data/ Computational Grids [6,18,51]	Cloud Platforms [1,9,11,12,30]
Architecture, Network Connectivity, and Size	Network of compute nodes interconnected by SAN, LAN, or WAN hierarchically	Flexible network of client machines logically connected by an overlay network	Heterogeneous clusters interconnected by high-speed network links over selected resource sites	Virtualized cluster of servers over data centers via SLA
Control and Resources Management	Homogeneous nodes with distributed control, running UNIX or Linux	Autonomous client nodes, free in and out, with self-organization	Centralized control, server-oriented with authenticated security	Dynamic resource provisioning of servers, storage, and networks
Applications and Network-centric Services	High-performance computing, search engines, and web services, etc.	Most appealing to business file sharing, content delivery, and social networking	Distributed supercomputing, global problem solving, and data center services	Upgraded web search, utility computing, and outsourced computing services
Representative Operational Systems	Google search engine, SunBlade, IBM Road Runner, Cray XT4, etc.	Gnutella, eMule, BitTorrent, Napster, KaZaA, Skype, JXTA	TeraGrid, GriPhyN, UK EGEE, D-Grid, ChinaGrid, etc.	Google App Engine, IBM Bluecloud, AWS, and Microsoft Azure

Computing cluster

- A computing cluster consists of interconnected stand-alone computers which work cooperatively as a single integrated computing resource.

Cluster Architecture

- the architecture consists of a typical server cluster built around a low-latency, high bandwidth interconnection network.
- build a larger cluster with more nodes, the interconnection network can be built with multiple levels of Gigabit Ethernet, Myrinet, or InfiniBand switches.
- Through hierarchical construction using a SAN, LAN, or WAN, one can build scalable clusters with an increasing number of nodes
- cluster is connected to the Internet via a virtual private network (VPN) gateway.
- gateway IP address locates the cluster

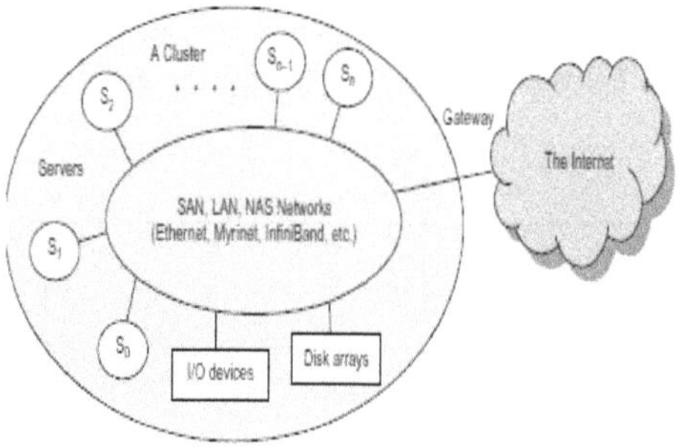

- Clusters have loosely coupled node computers.
- All resources of a server node are managed by their own OS.
- Most clusters have multiple system images as a result of having many autonomous nodes under different OS control

Single-System Image -Cluster

- an ideal cluster should merge multiple system images intoa single-system image (SSI)
- acluster operating system or some middleware have to support SSI at various levels, including the sharing of CPUs, memory, and I/O across all cluster nodes.
- illusion created by software or hardware that presents a collection of resources as one integrated, powerful resource
- SSI makes the cluster appear like a single machine to the user.
- A cluster with multiple system images is nothing but a collection ofindependent computers.

Hardware, Software, and Middleware Support –Cluster

- Clusters exploring massive parallelism are commonly known as MPPs –Massive Parallel Processing
- The building blocks are computer nodes (PCs, workstations, servers, or SMP), special communication software such as PVM or MPI, and a network interface card in each computer node.
- Most clusters run under the Linux OS.
- nodes are interconnected by a high-bandwidth network
- Special cluster middleware supports are needed to create SSI or high availability (HA).
- all distributed memory to be shared by all servers by forming distributed shared memory (DSM).
- SSI features are expensive
- achieving SSI, many clusters are loosely coupled machines
- virtual clusters are created dynamically, upon user demand

Grid Computing

- A web service such as HTTP enables remote access of remote web pages
- computing grid offers an infrastructure that couples computers, software/middleware, special instruments, and people and sensors together
- Enterprises or organizations present grids as integrated computing resources. They can also beviewed as virtual platforms to support virtual organizations.
- The computers used in a grid are primarilyworkstations, servers, clusters, and supercomputers

Peer-to-Peer Network-P2P

- P2P architecture offers a distributed model of networked systems.
- P2P network is client-oriented instead of server-oriented
- In a P2P system, every node acts as both a client and a server
- Peer machines are simply client computers connected to the Internet.
- All client machines act autonomously to join or leave the system freely. This implies that no master-slave relationship exists among the peers.
- No central coordination or central database is needed. The system is self-organizing with distributed control.
- P2P two layer of abstractions as given in the figure

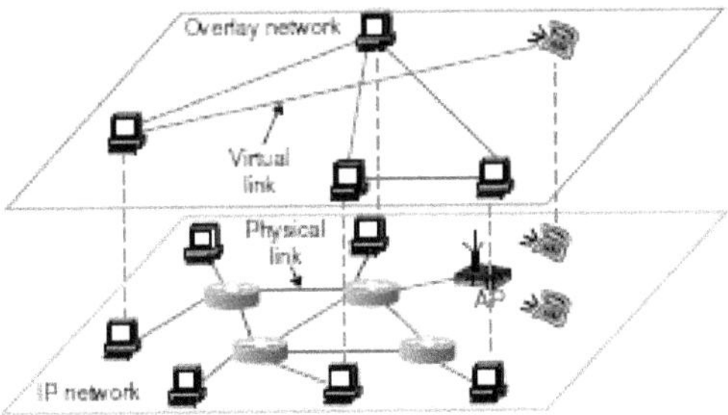

- Each peer machine joins or leaves the P2P network voluntarily
- Only the participatingpeers form the physical network at any time.
- Physical network is simply an ad hoc networkformed at various Internet domains randomly using the TCP/IP and NAI protocols.

Peer-to-Peer Network-Overlay network

- Data items or files are distributed in the participating peers.
- Based on communication or file-sharing needs, the peer IDs form an overlay network at the logical level.
- When a new peer joins the system, its peer ID is added as a node in the overlay network.
- When an existing peer leaves the system, its peer ID is removed from the overlay network automatically.
- An unstructured overlay network is characterized by a random graph. There is no fixed route to send messages or files among the nodes. Often, flooding is applied to send a query to all nodes in an unstructured overlay, thus resulting in heavy network traffic and nondeterministic search results.
- Structured overlay networks follow certain connectivity topology and rules for inserting and removing nodes (peer IDs) from the overlay graph

Cloud Computing

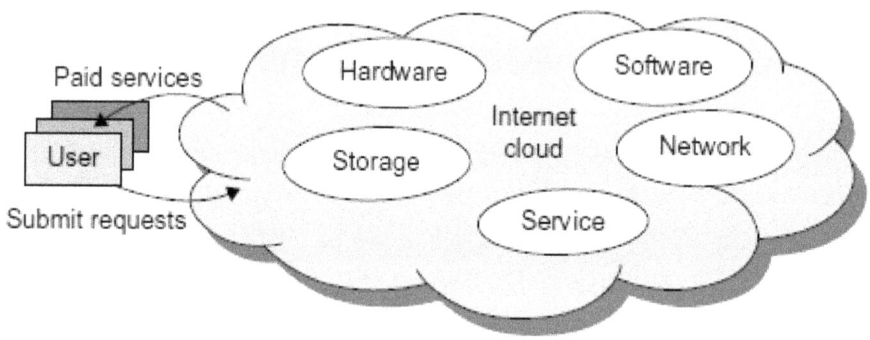

Virtualized resources from data centers to form an Internet cloud

- A cloud is a pool of virtualized computer resources.
- A cloud can host a variety of different workloads, including batch-style backend jobs and interactive and user-facing applications."
- Cloud computing applies a virtualized platform with elastic resources on demand by provisioning hardware, software, and data sets dynamically

The Cloud Landscape

Infrastructure as a Service (IaaS)

- This model puts together infrastructures demanded by users—namely servers, storage, networks, and the data center fabric.
- The user can deploy and run on multiple VMs running guest OSes on specific applications.
- The user does not manage or control the underlying cloud infrastructure, but can specify when to request and release the needed resources.

Platform as a Service (PaaS)

- This model enables the user to deploy user-built applications onto a virtualized cloud platform.
- PaaS includes middleware, databases, development tools, andsome runtime support such as Web 2.0 and Java.
- The platform includes both hardware andsoftware integrated with specific programming interfaces.
- The provider supplies the API andsoftware tools (e.g., Java, Python, Web 2.0, .NET). The user is freed from managing the cloudinfrastructure.

Software as a Service (SaaS)

- This refers to browser-initiated application software overthousands of paid cloud customers.
- The SaaS model applies to business processes, industryapplications, consumer relationship management (CRM), enterprise resources planning (ERP),human resources (HR), and collaborative applications.
- On the customer side, there is no upfrontinvestment in servers or software licensing.
- On the provider side, costs are rather low, comparedwith conventional hosting of user applications

Internet clouds offer four deployment modes: private, public, managed, and hybrid

SOFTWARE ENVIRONMENTS FOR DISTRIBUTED SYSTEMSAND CLOUDS

Service-Oriented Architecture (SOA)

- In grids/web services, Java, and CORBA, an entity is, respectively, a service, a Java object, and a CORBA distributed object in a variety of languages.
- These architectures build on the traditional seven Open Systems Interconnection (OSI) layers that provide the base networking abstractions.
- On top of this we have a base software environment, which would be
    - .NET or Apache Axis for web services,
    - the Java Virtual Machine for Java, and a broker network for CORBA
- On top of this base environment one would build a higher level environment reflecting the special features of the distributed computing environment.
- SOAapplies to building grids, clouds, grids of clouds, clouds of grids, clouds of clouds (also known asinterclouds),
- SS (sensor service : A large number of sensors provide data-collectionservices (ZigBee device, a Bluetoothdevice, WiFi access point, a personal computer, a GPA, or a wireless phoneetc
- Filter services : to eliminate unwanted raw data, in orderto respond to specific requests from the web, the grid, or web services

Layered Architecture for Web Services and Grids

- **Entity Interfaces**
- Java method interfaces correspond to the Web Services Description Language (WSDL),
- CORBA interface - definition language (IDL) specifications
- These interfaces are linked with customized, high-level communication systems: SOAP, RMI, and IIOP
- These communication systems support features including particular message patterns (such as Remote Procedure Call or RPC), fault recovery, and specialized routing.
- Communication systems are built on message-oriented middleware (enterprise bus) infrastructure such as Web-Sphere MQ or Java Message Service (JMS)

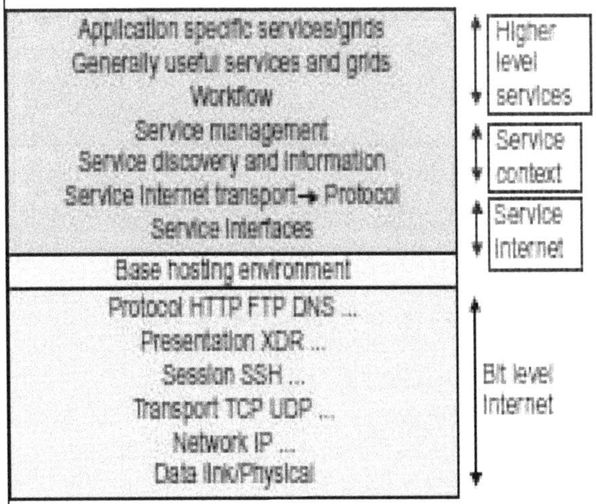

Cases of fault tolerance- the features in the Web Services Reliable Messaging (WSRM) Security -reimplements the capabilities seen in concepts such as Internet Protocol Security (IPsec)
Several models with, for example, JNDI (Jini and Java Naming and DirectoryInterface) illustrating different approaches within the Java distributed object model. The CORBA TradingService, UDDI (Universal Description, Discovery, and Integration), LDAP (Lightweight Directory Access Protocol), and ebXML (Electronic Business using eXtensibleMarkup Language
earlier years, CORBA and Java approaches were used in distributed systems rather than today'sSOAP, XML, or REST (Representational State Transfer).

Web Services and Tools

REST approach:

- delegates most ofthe difficult problems to application (implementation-specific) software. In a web services language
- minimal information in the header, and the message body (that is opaque to genericmessage processing) carries all the needed information.
- architectures are clearly more appropriatefor rapid technology environments.
- REST can use XML schemas but not those that are part of SOAP; "XML overHTTP" is a popular design choice in this regard.
- Above the communication and managementlayers, we have the ability to compose new entities or distributed programs by integrating severalentities together.

CORBA and Java:

- the distributed entities are linked with RPCs, and the simplest way to buildcomposite applications is to view the entities as objects and use the traditional ways of linking themtogether.
- For Java, this could be as simple as writing a Java program with method calls replaced byRemote Method Invocation (RMI),
- CORBA supports a similar model with a syntax reflecting theC++ style of its entity (object)

interfaces.

Parallel and Distributed Programming Models

Table 1.7 Parallel and Distributed Programming Models and Tool Sets

Model	Description	Features
MPI	A library of subprograms that can be called from C or FORTRAN to write parallel programs running on distributed computer systems [6,28,42]	Specify synchronous or asynchronous point-to-point and collective communication commands and I/O operations in user programs for message-passing execution
MapReduce	A web programming model for scalable data processing on large clusters over large data sets, or in web search operations [16]	*Map* function generates a set of intermediate key/value pairs; *Reduce* function merges all intermediate values with the same key
Hadoop	A software library to write and run large user applications on vast data sets in business applications (http://hadoop.apache.org/core)	A scalable, economical, efficient, and reliable tool for providing users with easy access of commercial clusters

PERFORMANCE, SECURITY, AND ENERGY EFFICIENCY

Performance Metrics:

- In a distributed system, performance is attributed to a large numberof factors.
- System throughput is often measured in MIPS, Tflops (tera floating-point operations persecond), or TPS (transactions per second).
- Systemoverhead is often attributed to OS boot time, compile time, I/O data rate, and the runtime support systemused.
- Other performance-related metrics include the QoS for Internet and web services; systemavailability and dependability; and security resilience for system defense against network attacks

Dimensions of Scalability

Any resource upgrade ina system should be backward compatible with existing hardware and software resources. System scaling can increase or decrease resources depending on many practicalfactors

Size scalability

- This refers to achieving higher performance or more functionality by increasingthe machine size.
- The word "size" refers to adding processors, cache, memory, storage, or I/Ochannels. The most obvious way to determine size scalability is to simply count the number ofprocessors installed.
- Not all parallel computer or distributed architectures are equally sizescalable.
- For example, the IBM S2 was scaled up to 512 processors in 1997. But in 2008, theIBMBlueGene/L system scaled up to 65,000 processors.

• **Software scalability**

- This refers to upgrades in the OS or compilers, adding mathematical andengineering libraries, porting new application software, and installing more user-friendlyprogramming environments.
- Some software upgrades may not work with large systemconfigurations.
- Testing and fine-tuning of new software on larger systems is a nontrivial job.

• **Application scalability**

- This refers to matching problem size scalability with machine sizescalability.
- Problem size affects the size of the data set or the workload increase. Instead of increasingmachine size, users can enlarge the problem size to enhance system efficiency or cost-effectiveness.

• **Technology scalability**

- This refers to a system that can adapt to changes in building technologies,such as the component and networking technologies
- Whenscaling a system design with new technology one must consider three aspects: time, space, andheterogeneity.
- (1) Time refers to generation scalability. When changing to new-generation processors,one must consider the impact to the motherboard, power supply, packaging and cooling,and so forth. Based on past experience, most systems upgrade their commodity processors everythree to five years.
- (2) Space is related to packaging and energy concerns. Technology scalabilitydemands

harmony and portability among suppliers.

- (3) Heterogeneity refers to the use ofhardware components or software packages from different vendors. Heterogeneity may limit thescalability.

Amdahl's Law

- Let the program has been parallelized or partitioned for parallel execution on a cluster of many processing nodes.
- Assume that a fraction α of the code must be executed sequentially, called the sequential bottleneck.
- Therefore, (1 − α) of the code can be compiled for parallel execution by n processors.

  The total execution time of the program is calculated byα T + (1 − α)T/n, where the first term is the sequential execution time on a single processor and the second term is the parallel execution time on n processing nodes.
- I/O time or exception handling time is also not included in the following speedup analysis.

$$\text{Speedup} = S = T/[\alpha T + (1-\alpha)T/n] = 1/[\alpha + (1-\alpha)/n]$$

- Amdahl's Law states that the speedup factor of using the n-processor system over the use of a single processor is expressed by:

- the code is fully parallelizable with α = 0. As the cluster becomes sufficiently large, that is, n → ∞, S approaches 1/α, an upper bound on the speedup S.

- this upper bound is independent of the cluster size n. The sequential bottleneck is the portion of the code that cannot be parallelized.

Gustafson's Law

- To achieve higher efficiency when using a large cluster, we must consider scaling the problem sizeto match the cluster capability. This leads to the following speedup law proposed by John Gustafson(1988), referred as scaled-workload speedup.

- Let W be the workload in a given program.

- When using an n-processor system, the user scales the workload to $W' = \alpha W + (1 - \alpha)nW$. Scaled workload W' is essentially the sequential execution time on a single processor. The parallelexecution time of a scaled workload W' on n processors is defined by a scaled-workload speedupas follows:

$$S = W'/W = [\alpha W + (1-\alpha)nW]/W = \alpha + (1-\alpha)n$$

Network Threats and Data Integrity

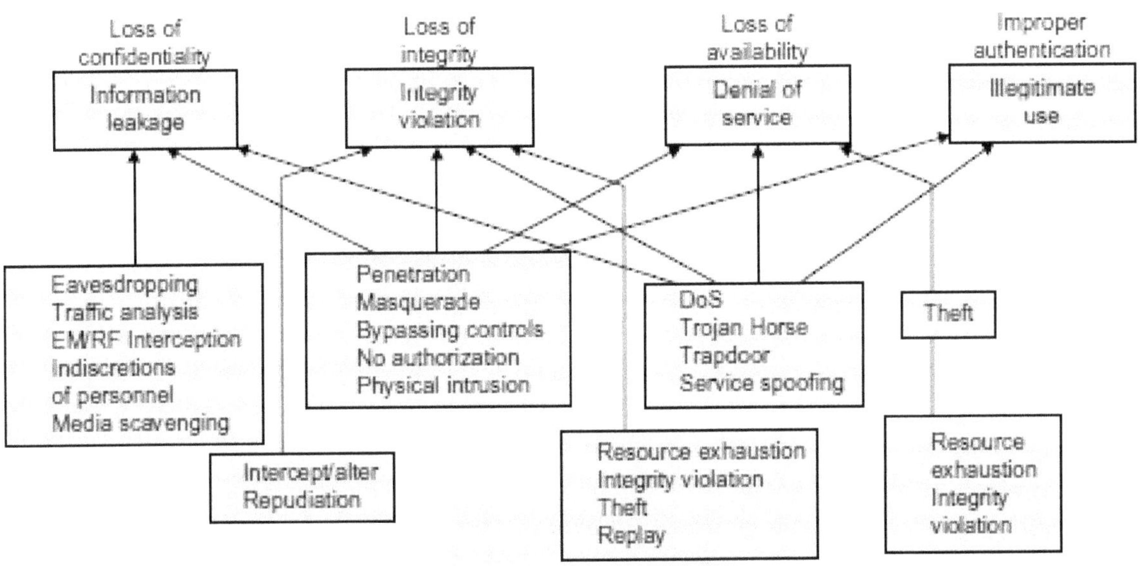

ENERGY EFFICIENCY IN DISTRIBUTED COMPUTING

Primary performance goals in conventional parallel and distributed computing systems are highperformance and high throughput, considering some form of performance reliability (e.g., fault toleranceand security). However, these systems recently encountered new challenging issues includingenergy efficiency, and workload and resource outsourcing

Energy Consumption of Unused Servers: To run a server farm (data center) a company has to spend a huge amount of money for hardware,software, operational support, and energy every year. Therefore, companies should thoroughlyidentify whether their installed server farm (more specifically, the volume of provisioned resources)is at an appropriate level, particularly in terms of utilization.

Reducing Energy in Active Servers: In addition to identifying unused/underutilized servers for energy savings, it is also necessary toapply appropriate techniques to decrease energy consumption in active distributed systems with negligibleinfluence on their performance.

Application Layer: Until now, most user applications in science, business, engineering, and financial areas tend toincrease a system's speed or quality. By introducing energy-aware applications, the challenge is todesign sophisticated multilevel and multi-domain energy management applications without hurtingperformance.

Middleware Layer: The middleware layer acts as a bridge between the application layer and the resource layer. Thislayer provides resource broker, communication service, task analyzer, task scheduler, securityaccess, reliability control, and information service capabilities. It is also responsible for applyingenergy-efficient techniques, particularly in task scheduling.

Resource Layer: The resource layer consists of a wide range of resources including computing nodes and storageunits. This layer generally interacts with hardware devices and the operating system; therefore, itis responsible for controlling all distributed resources in distributed computing systems. Dynamic power management (DPM) and dynamic voltage-frequency scaling (DVFS) are two popular methods incorporated into recent computer hardware systems. In DPM, hardware devices, such as the CPU, have the capability to switch from idle mode to one or more lower power modes. In DVFS, energy savings are achieved based on the fact that the power consumptionin CMOS circuits has a direct relationship with frequency and the square of the voltage supply.

Network Layer: Routing and transferring packets and enabling network services to the resource layer are the mainresponsibility of the network layer in distributed computing systems. The major challenge to buildenergy-efficient networks is, again, determining how to measure, predict, and create a balancebetween energy consumption and performance.

Clustering for Massive Parallelism

- A computer cluster is a collection of interconnected stand-alone computers which can work together collectively and cooperatively as a single integrated computing resource pool.
- Clustering explores massive parallelism at the job level and achieves high availability (HA) through stand-alone operations.
- Benefits of computer clusters and massively parallel processors (MPPs) include

- Scalable performance, HA, fault tolerance, modular growth, and use of commodity components. These features can sustain the generation changes experienced in hardware, software, and network components.

Design Objectives of Computer Clusters

Scalability:

- Clustering of computers is based on the concept of modular growth. To scale a cluster from hundreds of uniprocessor nodes to a supercluster with 10,000 multicore nodes is a nontrivial task.
- The scalability could be limited by a number of factors, such as the multicore chip technology, cluster topology, packaging method, power consumption, and cooling scheme applied.

Packaging

- Cluster nodes can be packaged in a compact or a slack fashion. In a compact cluster, the nodes are closely packaged in one or more racks sitting in a room, and the nodes are not attached to peripherals (monitors, keyboards, mice, etc.).
- In a slack cluster, the nodes are attached to their usual peripherals (i.e., they are complete

SMPs, workstations, and PCs), and they may be located in different rooms, different buildings, or even remote regions.

- Packaging directly affects communication wire length, and thus the selection of interconnection technology used.
- While a compact cluster can utilize a high-bandwidth, low-latency communication network that is often proprietary, nodes of a slack cluster are normally connected through standard LANs or WANs.

Control

- A cluster can be either controlled or managed in a centralized or decentralized fashion. A compact cluster normally has centralized control, while a slack cluster can be controlled either way.
- In a centralized cluster, all the nodes are owned, controlled, managed, and administered by a central operator.
- In a decentralized cluster, the nodes have individual owners. This lack of a single point of control makes system administration of such a cluster very difficult. It also calls for special techniques for process scheduling, workload migration, checkpointing, accounting, and other similar tasks.

Homogeneity

- A homogeneous cluster uses nodes from the same platform, that is, the same processor architecture and the same operating system; often, the nodes are from the same vendors.
- A heterogeneous cluster uses nodes of different platforms. Interoperability is an important issue in heterogeneous clusters.
- In a homogeneous cluster, a binary process image can migrate to another node and continue execution.
- This is not feasible in a heterogeneous cluster, as the binary code will not be executable when the process migrates to a node of a different platform.

Security

- Intracluster communication can be either exposed or enclosed.
- In an exposed cluster, the communication paths among the nodes are exposed to the outside world. An outside machine can access the communication paths, and thus individual nodes, using standard protocols (e.g., TCP/IP).
- Such exposed clusters are easy to implement, but have several disadvantages:

  • Being exposed, intracluster communication is not secure, unless the communication subsystemperforms additional work to ensure privacy and security.

- Outside communications may disrupt intracluster communications in an unpredictable fashion.
- Standard communication protocols tend to have high overhead.
- In an enclosed cluster, intracluster communication is shielded from the outside world, which
- alleviates the aforementioned problems.
- A disadvantage is that there is currently no standard for efficient, enclosed intracluster communication. Consequently, most commercial or academic clusters realize fast communications through one-of-a-kind protocols

Fundamental Cluster Design Issues

1. **Scalable Performance:** Scaling of resources (cluster nodes, memory capacity, I/O bandwidth, etc.) leads to a proportional increase in performance. Both scale-up and scale-down capabilities are needed, depending on application demand or cost-effectiveness considerations. Clustering is driven by scalability

2. **Single-System Image (SSI):** A set of workstations connected by an Ethernet network is not necessarily a cluster. A cluster is a single system.

3. **Availability Support:** Clusters can provide cost-effective HA capability with lots of redundancy in processors, memory, disks, I/O devices, networks, and operating system

images

4. **Cluster Job Management:** Clusters try to achieve high system utilization from traditional workstations or PC nodes that are normally not highly utilized. Job management software is required to provide batching, load balancing, parallel processing, and other functionality

5. **Inter node Communication:** The inter node physical wire lengths are longer in a cluster than in an MPP. A long wire implies greater interconnect network latency. But, longer wires have more problems in terms of reliability, clock skew, and cross talking. These problems call for reliable and secure communication protocols, which increase overhead. Clusters often use commodity networks (e.g., Ethernet) with standard protocols such as TCP/IP.

6. **Fault Tolerance and Recovery:** Clusters of machines can be designed to eliminate all single points of failure. Through redundancy, a cluster can tolerate faulty conditions up to a certain extent. Heartbeat mechanisms can be installed to monitor the running condition of all nodes. In case of a node failure, critical jobs running on the failing nodes can be saved by failing over to the surviving node machines. Rollback recovery schemes restore the computing results through periodic checkpointing.

7. **Cluster Family Classification:**computer clusters are divided into three classes

- **Compute clusters:**
    - These are clusters designed mainly for collective computationover a single large job. The compute clusters do not handle many I/O operations, such as database services. When a single compute job requires frequent communication among the cluster nodes, the cluster must share a dedicated network, and thus the nodes are mostly homogeneous and tightly coupled. This type of clusters is also known as a **Beowulf cluster**

- **High-Availability clusters** HA (high-availability)
    - clusters are designed to be fault-tolerant and achieve HA of services. HA clusters operate with many redundant nodes to sustain faults or failures.
- **Load-balancing clusters**
    - These clusters shoot for higher resource utilization through load balancing among all participating nodes in the cluster. All nodes share the workload or function as a single virtual machine (VM).
    - Requests initiated from the user are distributed to all node computers to form a cluster. This results in a balanced workload among different machines, and thus higher resource utilization or higher performance. Middleware is needed to achieve dynamic load balancing by job or process migration among all the cluster nodes

Basic Cluster Architecture

- simple cluster of computers built with commodity components supported with desired SSI features and HA capability
- commodity nodes are easy to replace or upgrade with new generations of hardware
- node operating systems should be designed for multiuser, multitasking, and multithreaded applications.
- nodes are interconnected by one or more fast commodity networks and use standard communication protocols
- network interface card is connected to the node's standard I/O bus

<table>
<tr><td rowspan="3">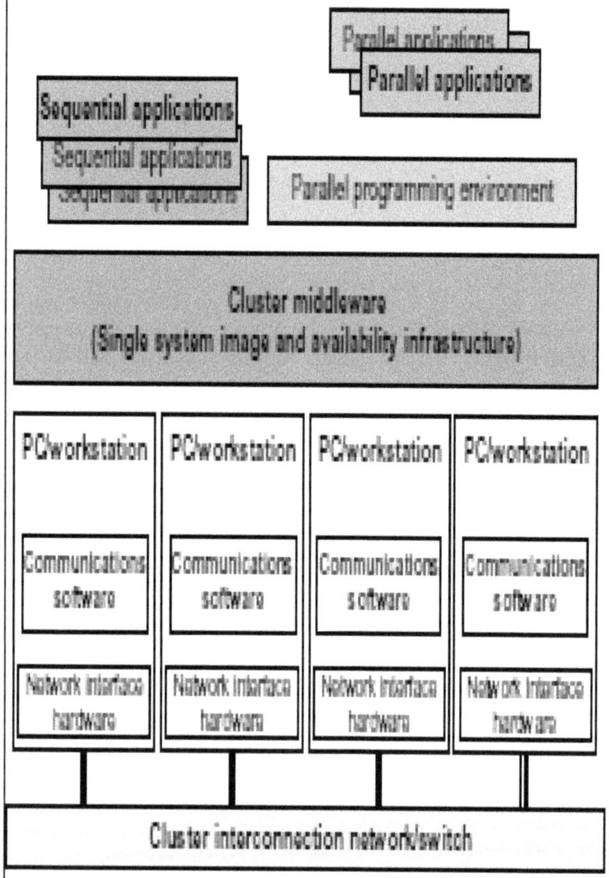
</td><td>When the processor or the operating system is changed, only the driver software needs to change.</td></tr>
<tr><td>a cluster OS is not commercially available. Instead, we can deploy some cluster middleware to glue together all node platforms at the user space</td></tr>
<tr><td>• middleware offers HA services
• An SSI layer provides a single entry point, a single file hierarchy, a single point of control
• idealized cluster is supported by three subsystems
• conventional databasesand OLTP monitors
• A user interface subsystemis needed to combine the advantages of the web interface and the Windows GUI.
• cluster supports parallel programming based on standard languages and communication libraries using PVM, MPI, or OpenMP. The programming environment also includes tools for debugging, profiling, monitoring</td></tr>
</table>

Resource Sharing in Clusters

Clustering improves both availability and performance. Some HA clusters use hardware redundancy for scalable performance. The nodes of a cluster can be connected in one of three ways

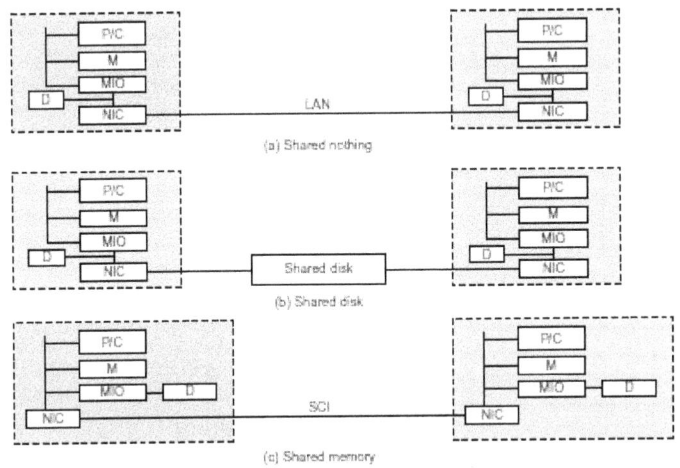

Part (a) simply connects two or more autonomous computers via a LAN such as Ethernet.

Part (b): shared-disk cluster

Part (c) shared-memory cluster

DESIGN PRINCIPLES OF COMPUTER CLUSTERS

General-purpose computers and clusters of cooperative computers should be designed for scalability, availability, Single System Image, High Availability, Fault tolerance, and Rollback recovery

- **Single System Image**: A single system image is the illusion, created by software or hardware, that presents a collection of resources as an integrated powerful resource. SSI makes the cluster appear like a single machine to the user, applications, and network. A cluster with multiple system images is nothing but a collection of independent computers **Single-System-Image Features**
    - **Single System**: The entire cluster is viewed by the users as one system, which has multiple processors.
    - **Single Control**: Logically, an end user or system user utilizes services from one place with a single interface.
    - **Symmetry**: A user can use a cluster service from any node. All cluster services and functionalities are symmetric to all nodes and all users, except those protected by access rights.
    - **Location Transparent**: The user is not aware of the whereabouts of the physical device

that eventually provides a service.

Basic SSI Services

A. Single Entry Point

telnet cluster.usc.edu

telnet node1.cluster.usc.edu

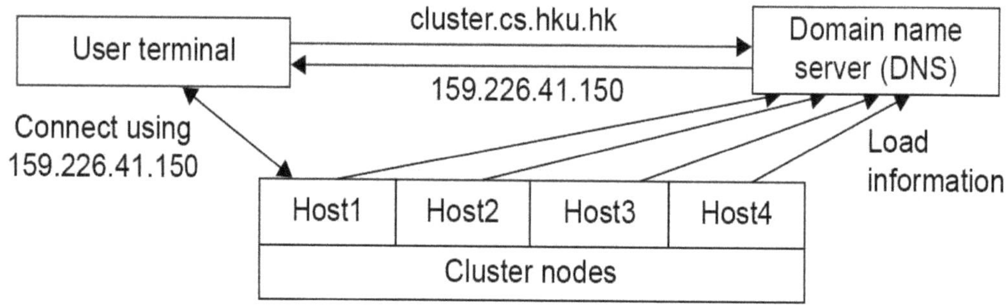

1. Four nodes of a cluster are used as host nodes to receive users' login requests.
2. To log into the cluster a standard Unix command such as "telnet cluster.cs.hku.hk", using the symbolic name of the cluster system is issued.
3. The symbolic name is translated by the DNS, which returns with the IP address 159.226.41.150 of the least-loaded node, which happens to be node Host1.
4. The user then logs in using this IP address.
5. The DNS periodically receives load information from the host nodes to make load-balancing translation decisions.

B. Single File Hierarchy: xFS, AFS, Solaris MC Proxy

The illusion of a single, huge file system image that transparently integrates local and global disks and other file devices (e.g., tapes). Files can reside on 3 types of locations in a cluster:

Local storage - disk on the local node.

Remote storage - disks on remote nodes.

Stable storage -

Persistent - data, once written to the stable storage, will stay there at least for a period of time (e.g., a week), even after the cluster shuts down.

Fault tolerant - to some degree, by using redundancy and periodical backup to tapes.

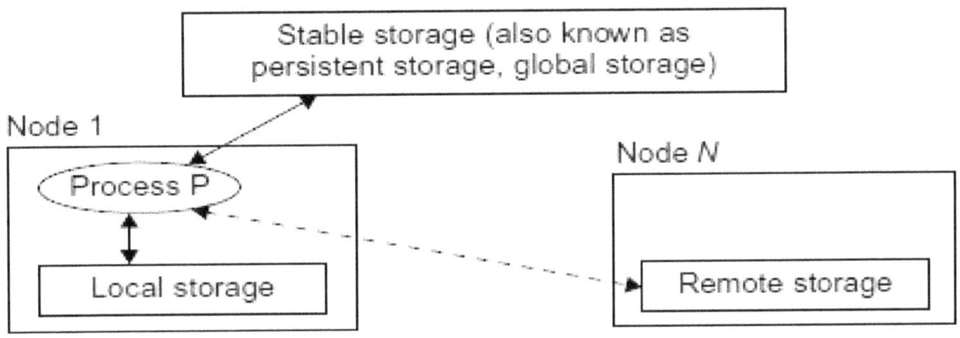

Three types of storage in a single file hierarchy. Solid lines show what process P can access and thedashed line shows what P may be able to access

C. **Single I/O, Networking, and Memory Space:** To achieve SSI, we need a:

- single control point
- single address space
- single job management system
- single user interface
- single process control

Single Networking: A properly designed cluster should behave as one system. Any process on any node can use any network and I/O device as though it were attached to the local node. Single networking means any node can access any network connection.

Single Point of Control: The system administrator should be able to configure, monitor, test, and control the entire cluster and each individual node from a single point. Many clusters help with this through a system console that is connected to all nodes of the cluster

Single Memory Space: Single memory space gives users the illusion of a big, centralized main memory, which in reality may be a set of distributed local memory spaces.

Single I/O Address Space: A single I/O space implies that any node can access the RAIDs

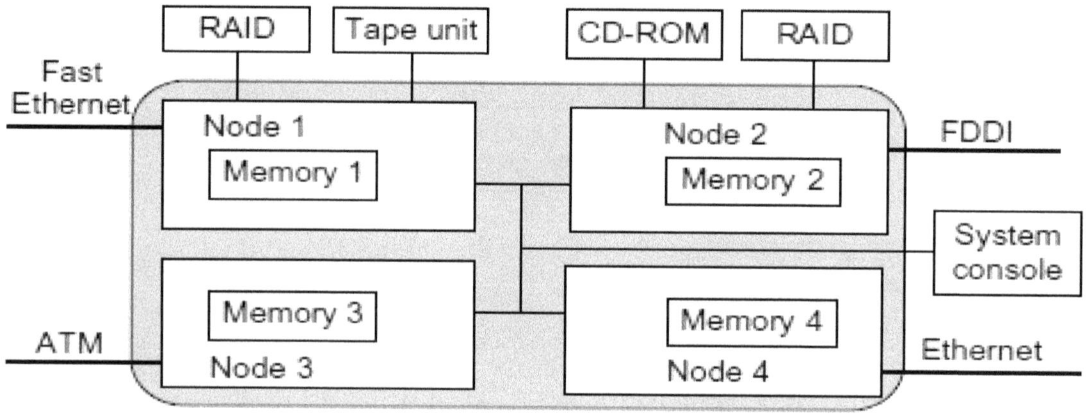

A cluster with single networking, single I/O space, single memory, and single point of control

Other Services

Single Job Management: All cluster jobs can be submitted from any node to a single job management system. GlUnix, Codine, LSF, etc.

Single User Interface: The users use the cluster through a single graphical interface. Such an interface is available for workstations and PCs like CDE in Solaris/NT

Single process space All user processes created on various nodes form a single process space and share a uniform process identification scheme. A process on any node can create(e.g., through a UNIX fork) or communicate with (e.g., through signals, pipes, etc.) processes on remote nodes.

Middleware support for SSI clusteringSSI features aresupported by middleware developed at three cluster application levels:

• **Management level** This level handles user applications and provides a job management system such as GLUnix, MOSIX, Load Sharing Facility (LSF), or Codine.

• **Programming level**This level provides single file hierarchy (NFS, xFS, AFS, Proxy) and distributed shared memory (TreadMark, Wind Tunnel).

• **Implementation level** This level supports a single process space, checkpointing, process migration, and a single I/O space. These features must interface with the cluster hardware and OS platform.

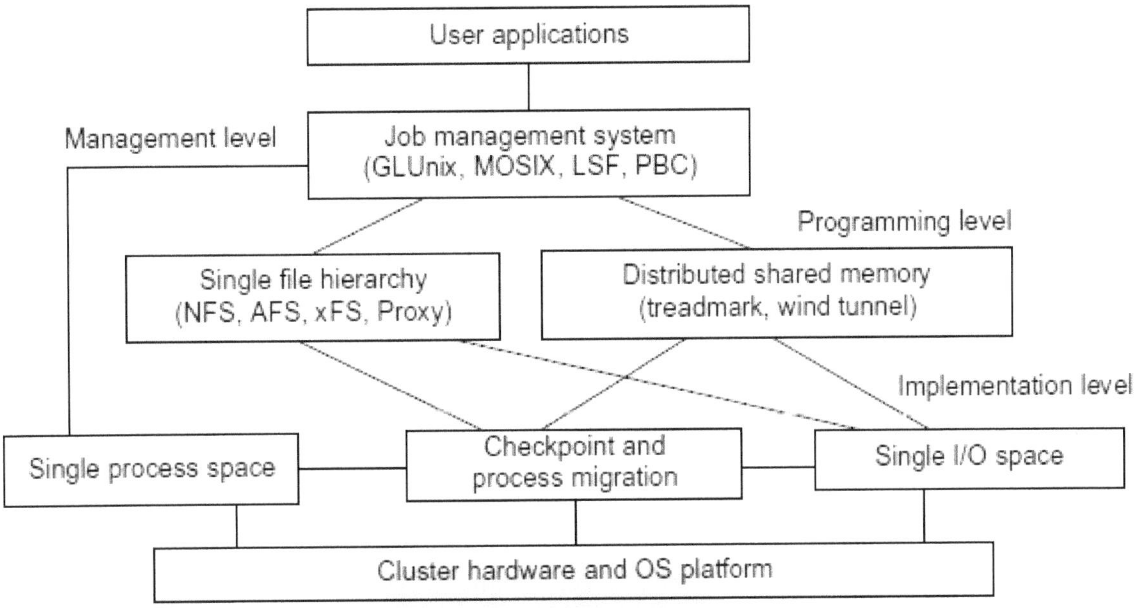

Relationship among clustering middleware at the job management, programming, and implementation levels.

- **High Availability through Redundancy:**

  - **Reliability** measures how long a system can operate without a breakdown.
  - **Availability** indicates the percentage of time that a system is available to the user, that is, thepercentage of system uptime.

• **Serviceability** refers to how easy it is to service the system, including hardware and softwaremaintenance, repair, upgrades, and so on.

A system's reliability is measured by the mean time to failure (MTTF), which is the average time of normal operation before the system (or a component of the system) fails. The metricfor serviceability is the mean time to repair (MTTR), which is the average time it takes to repair thesystem and restore it to working condition after it fails.

The availability of a system is defined by:

Availability = MTTF/ (MTTF +MTTR)

Failure is any event that prevents the system from normal operation

- **Unplanned failures** The system breaks, due to an operating system crash, a hardware failure, anetwork disconnection, human operation errors, a power outage, and so on. All these are simplycalled failures. The system must be repaired to correct the failure.
- **Planned shutdowns**The system is not broken, but is periodically taken off normal operationfor upgrades, reconfiguration, and maintenance.

Transient versus Permanent Failures

A lot of failures are **transient** in that they occur temporarily and then disappear. They can be dealtwith without replacing any components. A standard approach is to roll back the system to a known state and start over.

Permanent failures cannot be corrected by rebooting. Some hardwareor software component must be repaired or replaced. For instance, rebooting will not work ifthe system hard disk is broken.

Partial versus Total Failures

A failure that renders the entire system unusable is called a **total** failure. A failure that only affectspart of the system is called a **partial** failure if the system is still usable, even at a reduced capacity

Redundancy Techniques

Isolated Redundancy: A key technique to improve availability in any system is to use redundant components. When acomponent (the primary component) fails, the service it provided is taken over by another component(the backup component). Furthermore, the primary and the backup components should be isolatedfrom each other, meaning they should not be subject to the same cause of failure. Clustersprovide HA with redundancy in power supplies, fans, processors, memories, disks, I/O devices, networks,operating system images, and so on. In a carefully designed cluster, redundancy is also isolated.

N-Version Programming to Enhance Software Reliability

A common isolated-redundancy approach to constructing a mission-critical software system is calledN-version programming. The software is implemented by N isolated teams who may not even knowthe others exist. Different teams are asked to implement the software using different algorithms,programming languages, environment tools, and even platforms In a fault-tolerant system, the N versions all run simultaneously and their results are constantly compared. If the results differ, thesystem is notified that a fault has occurred.

- **Fault-Tolerant Cluster Configurations:** The cluster solution was targeted to provide availability support for two server nodes with threeascending levels of availability: hot standby, active takeover, and fault-tolerant. The level of availabilityincreases from standby to active and fault-tolerant cluster configurations. The shorter is the recoverytime, the higher is the cluster availability. Failback refers to the ability of a recovered node returningto normal operation after repair or maintenance. Activeness refers to whether the node is used inactive work during normal operation.

- **Hot standby server clusters**: In a hot standby cluster, only the primary node is activelydoing all the useful work normally. The standby node is powered on (hot) and running some monitoring programs to communicate heartbeat signals to check the status of the primary node, but is not actively running other useful workloads. The primary node must mirror any data to shared disk storage, which is accessible by the standby node. The standby node requires a second copy of data.
- **Active-takeover clusters**: In this case, the architecture is symmetric among multiple server nodes. Both servers are primary, doing useful work normally. Both failover and failback are often supported on both server nodes. When a node fails, the user applications fail over to the available node in the cluster. Depending on the time required to implement the failover,

users may experience some delays or may lose some data that was not saved in the last checkpoint.

- **Failover cluster:** When a component fails, this technique allows the remaining system to take over the services originally provided by the failed component. A failover mechanism mustprovide several functions, such as failure diagnosis, failure notification, and failure recovery.Failure diagnosis refers to the detection of a failure and the location of the failed componentthat caused the failure. A commonly used technique is heartbeat, whereby the cluster nodessend out a stream of heartbeat messages to one another. If the system does not receive thestream of heartbeat messages from a node, it can conclude that either the node or the networkconnection has failed.

Recovery Schemes

Failure recovery refers to the actions needed to take over the workload of a failed component. Thereare two types of recovery techniques. In **backward recovery**, the processes running on a cluster periodicallysave a consistent state (called a checkpoint) to a stable storage. After a failure, the systemis reconfigured to isolate the failed component, restores the previous checkpoint, and resumes normaloperation. This is called rollback. Backward recovery is relatively easy to implement in an application-independent, portable fashion

If execution time is crucial,such as in real-time systems where the rollback time cannot be tolerated, a **forward recovery** schemeshould be used. With such a scheme, the system is not rolled back to the previous checkpoint upon afailure. Instead, the system utilizes the failure diagnosis information to reconstruct a valid system stateand continues execution. Forward recovery is application-dependent and may need extra hardware

Checkpointing and Recovery Techniques

Checkpointingisthe process of periodically saving the state of an executing program to stable storage, from whichthe system can recover after a failure. Each program state saved is called a checkpoint. The disk filethat contains the saved state is called the checkpoint file.

Checkpointing techniques are useful not only for availability, but also for program debugging, process migration, and load balancing

Checkpointing can be realized by the operating system at the **kernel level**, where the OS transparentlycheckpoints and restarts processes
A less transparent approach linksthe user code with a checkpointing**library in the user space**. Checkpointing and restarting are handled by this runtime support. This approach is used widely because it has the advantage thatuser applications do not have to be modified.

A third approach requires the **user (or the compiler)** to insert checkpointingfunctions in the application; thus, the application has to be modified, and the transparencyis lost. However, it has the advantage that the user can specify where to checkpoint. This is helpful to reduce checkpointing overhead. Checkpointing incurs both time and storage overheads.

Checkpoint Overheads
During a program's execution, its states may be saved many times. This is denoted by the time consumedto save one checkpoint. The storage overhead is the extra memory and disk space requiredfor checkpointing. Both time and storage overheads depend on the size of the checkpoint file.

Choosing an Optimal Checkpoint Interval

The time period between two checkpoints is called the checkpoint interval. Making the interval larger can reduce checkpoint time overhead.
Wong and Franklin derived an expression for optimal checkpoint interval
Optimal checkpoint interval = Square root (MTTF x t_c)/h
MTTF is the system's mean time to failure. This MTTF accounts the time consumed to save one checkpoint, and h is the average percentage of normal computation performed in a checkpointinterval before the system fails. The parameter h is always in the range. After a system isrestored, it needs to spend h × (checkpoint interval) time to recompute.

Incremental Checkpoint

Instead of saving the full state at each checkpoint, an incremental checkpoint scheme saves only theportion of the state that is changed from the previous checkpoint In full-state checkpointing, only one checkpoint file needs to be kepton disk. Subsequent checkpoints simply overwrite this file. With incremental checkpointing, old filesneeded to be kept, because a state may span many files. Thus, the total storage requirement is larger

Forked Checkpointing

Most checkpoint schemes are blocking in that the normal computation is stopped while checkpointingis in progress. With enough memory, checkpoint overhead can be reduced by making a copy ofthe program state in memory and invoking another asynchronous thread to perform the checkpointingconcurrently. A simple way to overlap checkpointing with computation is to use the UNIXfork( ) system call. The forked child process duplicates the parent process's address space andcheckpoints it. Meanwhile, the parent process continues execution. Overlapping is achieved sincecheckpointing is disk-I/O intensive

User-Directed Checkpointing

The checkpoint overheads can sometimes be substantially reduced if the user inserts code (e.g., library or system calls) to tell the system when to save, what to save, and what not to save. What should be the exact contents of a checkpoint? It should contain just enough information to allow asystem to recover. The state of a process includes its data state and control state

Checkpointing Parallel Programs The state of a parallel program is usually much larger than that of a sequential program, as it consists of the set of the states of individual processes, plus thestate of the communication network. Parallelism also introduces various timing and consistency problems

Consistent Snapshot

A global snapshot is called consistent if there is no message that is received by the checkpoint of one process, but not yet sent by another process. Graphically, this corresponds to the case that no arrow crosses a snapshot line from right to left

Coordinated versus Independent Checkpointing

Checkpointing schemes for parallel programs can be classified into two types. In coordinated checkpointing(also called consistent checkpointing), the parallel program is frozen, and all processes arecheckpointed at the same time. In independent checkpointing, the processes are checkpointed independentof one another.

Cluster Job Scheduling and Management

A Job Management System (*JMS*) should have three parts:

- A **user server** lets the user submit jobs to one or more queues, specify resource requirements for each job, delete a job from a queue, inquire about the status of a job or a queue.
- A **job scheduler** that performs job scheduling and queuing according to job types, resource requirements, resource availability, and scheduling policies.
- A **resource manager** that allocates and monitors resources, enforces scheduling policies, and collects accounting information.

JMS Administration

- JMS should be able to dynamically reconfigure the cluster with minimal impact on the running jobs.
- The administrator's prologue and epilogue scripts should be able to run before and after each job for security checking, accounting, and cleanup.
- Users should be able to cleanly kill their own jobs.
- The administrator or the JMS should be able to cleanly suspend or kill any job.
  - Clean means that when a job is suspended or killed, all its processes must be included.
  - Otherwise some "orphan" processes are left in the system, wasting cluster resources and may eventually render the system unusable.

Several types of jobs execute on a cluster.

- Serial jobs run on a single node.
- Parallel jobs use multiple nodes.
- Interactive jobs are those that require fast turnaround time, and their input/output is directed to a terminal.
    - These jobs do not need large resources, and the users expect them to execute immediately, not made to wait in a queue.
- Batch jobs normally need more resources, such as large memory space and long CPU time.
    - But they do not need immediate response.
    - They are submitted to a job queue to be scheduled to run when the resource becomes available (e.g., during off hours).

Multi-Job Scheduling Schemes

- Cluster jobs may be scheduled to run at a specific time (**calendar scheduling**) or when a particular event happens (**event scheduling**).
- Jobs are scheduled according to priorities based on submission time, resource nodes, execution time, memory, disk, job type, and user identity.
- With **static priority**, jobs are assigned priorities according to a predetermined, fixed scheme.
    - A simple scheme is to schedule jobs in a first-come, first-serve fashion.
    - Another scheme is to assign different priorities to users.

With **dynamic priority**, the priority of a job may change over time.

Issue	Scheme	Key Problems
Job priority	**Non-preemptive**	Delay of high-priority jobs
	Preemptive	Overhead, implementation
Resource required	**Static**	Load imbalance
	Dynamic	Overhead, implementation
Resource sharing	**Dedicated**	Poor utilization
	Space sharing	Tiling, large job
Scheduling	**Time sharing**	Process-based job control with context switch overhead
	Independent	Severe slowdown
	Gang scheduling	Implementation difficulty
Competing with foreign (local) jobs	**Stay**	Local job slowdown
	Migrate	Migration threshold, Migration overhead

Job Scheduling Issues and Schemes for Cluster Nodes

Scheduling Modes

Dedicated Mode:

- Only one job runs in the cluster at a time, and at most one process of the job is assigned to a node at a time.
- The single job runs until completion before it releases the cluster to run other jobs.

Space Sharing:

Multiple jobs can run on disjoint partitions (groups) of nodes simultaneously.

- At most one process is assigned to a node at a time.
- Although a partition of nodes is dedicated to a job, the interconnect and the I/O subsystem may be shared by all jobs.

Time sharing :

- Multiple user processes are assigned to the same node.

Time-sharing introduces the following parallel scheduling policies:

- **Independent Scheduling (Independent):** Uses the operating system ofeach cluster node to schedule different processes as in a traditional workstation.
- **Gang Scheduling**: Schedules all processes of a parallel job together. When one process is active, all processes are active.
- **Competition with Foreign (Local) Jobs**: Scheduling becomes more complicated when both cluster jobs and local jobs are running. The local jobs should have priority over cluster jobs.

1. **Migration Scheme IssuesNode Availability**: Can the job find another available node to migrate to?

   - Berkeley study : Even during peak hours, 60% of workstations in a cluster are available.

2. **Migration Overhead**: The migration time can significantly slow down a parallel job.
   - Berkeley study : a slowdown as great as 2.4 times.
   - Slowdown is less if a parallel job is run on a cluster of twice the size.
   - e.g. a 32-node job on a 60-node cluster – migration slowdown no more than 20%, even when migration time of 3 minutes.

3. **Recruitment Threshold**: the amount of time a workstation stays unused before the cluster considers it an idle node.

UNIT -2

Levels of Virtualization Implementation

- Virtualization is a computer architecture technology by which multiple virtual machines (VMs) aremultiplexed in the same hardware machine.
- After virtualization, different user applications managed by their own operating systems (guest OS) can run onthe same hardware independent of the host OS
- done by adding additional software, called a virtualization layer
- This virtualization layer is known as hypervisor or virtual machine monitor (VMM)

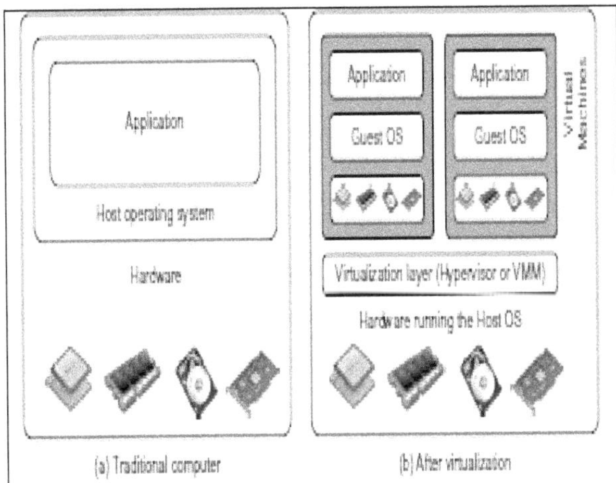

FIGURE 3.1

The architecture of a computer system before and after virtualization, where VMM stands for virtual machine monitor.

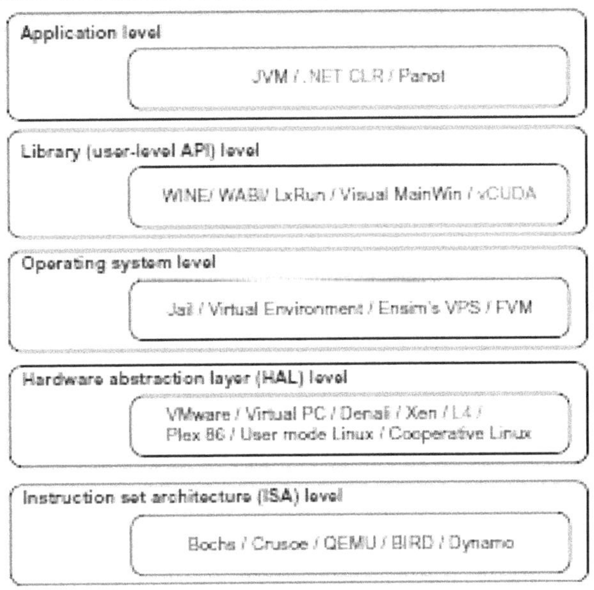

- function of the software layer for virtualization is to virtualize the physical hardware of a ost machine into virtual resources to be used by the VMs
- Common virtualization layers include the instruction set architecture (ISA) level, hardware level, operating system level, library support level, and application level

Instruction Set Architecture Level

- At the ISA level, virtualization is performed by emulating a given ISA by the ISA of the host machine. For example, MIPS binary code can run on an x86-based host machine with the help of ISA emulation. With this approach, it is possible to run a large amount of legacy binary code written for various processors on any given new hardware host machine.

- Instruction set emulation leads to virtual ISAs created on any hardware machine. The basic emulation method is through code interpretation. An interpreter program interprets the source instructions to target instructions one by one. One source instruction may require tens or hundreds of native target instructions to perform its function. Obviously, this process is relatively slow. For better performance, dynamic binary translation is desired.
- This approach translates basic blocks of dynamic source instructions to target instructions. The basic blocks can also be extended to program traces or super blocks to increase translation efficiency.
- Instruction set emulation requires binary translation and optimization. A virtual instruction set architecture (V-ISA) thus requires adding a processor-specific software translation layer to the compiler.

Hardware Abstraction Level

- Hardware-level virtualization is performed right on top of the bare hardware.
- Thisapproach generates a virtual hardware environment for a VM.
- The process managesthe underlying hardware through virtualization. The idea is to virtualize a computer's resources, such asits processors, memory, and I/O devices.
- The intention is to upgrade the hardware utilization rate bymultiple users concurrently. The idea was implemented in the IBM VM/370 in the 1960s.
- Morerecently, the Xen hypervisor has been applied to virtualize x86-based machines to run Linux or otherguest OS applications.

Operating System Level

- This refers to an abstraction layer between traditional OS and user applications.
- OS-level virtualizationcreates isolated containers on a single physical server and the OS instances to utilize the hardwareand software in data centers.
- The containers behave like real servers.
- OS-level virtualization iscommonly used in creating virtual hosting environments to allocate hardware resources among alarge number of mutually distrusting users.
- It is also used, to a lesser extent, in consolidating serverhardware by moving services on separate hosts into containers or VMs on one server.

Library Support Level

- Most applications use APIs exported by user-level libraries rather than using lengthy system callsby the OS.
- Since most systems provide well-documented APIs, such an interface becomes anothercandidate for virtualization.
- Virtualization with library interfaces is possible by controlling the communicationlink between applications and the rest of a system through API hooks.

User-Application Level

- Virtualization at the application level virtualizes an application as a VM.
- On a traditional OS, anapplication often runs as a process. Therefore, application-level virtualization is also known as process-level virtualization.
- The most popular approach is to deploy high level language (HLL)VMs. In this scenario, the virtualization layer sits as an application program on top of the operatingsystem,
- The layer exports an abstraction of a VM that can run programs written and compiledto a particular abstract machine definition.
- Any program written in the HLL and compiled for thisVM will be able to run on it. The Microsoft .NET CLR and Java Virtual Machine (JVM) are twogood examples of this class of VM.

VMM Design Requirements and Providers

- layer between real hardware and traditional operating systems. This layer is commonly called the Virtual Machine Monitor (VMM)
- three requirements for a VMM
- a VMM should provide an environment for programs which is essentially identical to the original machine
- programs run in this environment should show, at worst, only minor decreases in speed
- VMM should be in complete control of the system resources.
- VMM includes the following aspects:
- (1) The VMM is responsible for allocating hardware resources for programs;
- (2) it is not possible for a program to access any resource not explicitly allocated to it;

- (3) it is possible under certain circumstances for a VMM to regain control of resources already allocated.

Virtualization Support at the OS Level

- Why OS-Level Virtualization? :
    - it is slow to initialize a hardware-level VM because each VM creates its own image from scratch.
- OS virtualization inserts a virtualization layer inside an operating system to partition a machine's physical resources.
- It enables multiple isolated VMs within a single operating system kernel.
- This kind of VM is often called a virtual execution environment (VE), Virtual Private System (VPS), or simply container
- The benefits of OS extensions are twofold:
    - (1) VMs at the operating system level have minimal startup/shutdown costs, low resource requirements, and high scalability;
    - (2) for an OS-level VM, it is possible for a VM and its host environment to synchronize state changes when necessary.

Middleware Support for Virtualization

- Library-level virtualization is also known as user-level Application Binary Interface (ABI) or API emulation.
- This type of virtualization can create execution environments for running alien programs on a platform

Hypervisor and Xen Architecture

- The hypervisor software sits directly between the physical hardware and its OS.
- This virtualization layer is referred to as either the VMM or the hypervisor

Xen Architecture

- Xen is an open source hypervisor program developed by Cambridge University.
- Xen is a microkernel hypervisor

- The core components of a Xen system are the hypervisor, kernel, and applications
- The **guest OS**, which has control ability, is called **Domain 0**, and the others are called **Domain U**
- Domain 0 is designed to access hardware directly and manage devices

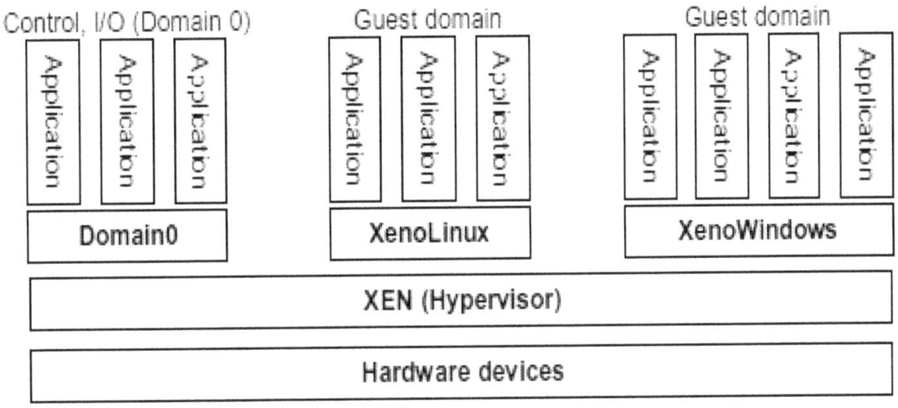

FIGURE 3.5

The Xen architecture's special domain 0 for control and I/O, and several guest domains for user applications.

(Courtesy of P. Barham, et al. [7])

- VM state is akin to a tree: the current state of the machine is a point that progresses monotonically as the software executes.
- VMs are allowed to roll back to previous states in their execution (e.g., to fix configuration errors) or rerun from the same point many times

Full virtualization

- Full virtualization, noncritical instructions run on the hardware directly while critical instructions are discovered and replaced with traps into the VMM to be emulated by software
- **VMware** puts the **VMM at Ring 0** and the **guest OS at Ring 1**.
- The VMM scans the instruction stream and identifies the privileged, control- and behavior-sensitive instructions.
- When these instructions are identified, they are trapped into the VMM, which emulates the behavior of these instructions.

- The method used in this emulation is called binary translation.
- Therefore, **full virtualization combines binary translation and direct execution.**

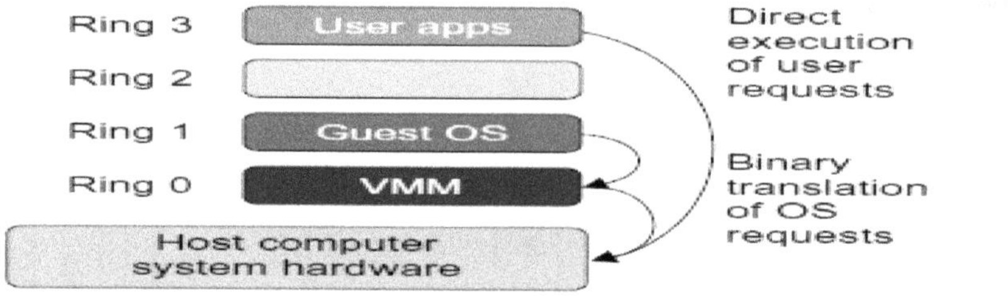

FIGURE 3.6

Indirect execution of complex instructions via binary translation of guest OS requests using the VMM plus direct execution of simple instructions on the same host.

(Courtesy of VM Ware [71])

Para-Virtualization

- Para-virtualization needs to modify the guest operating systems
- A para-virtualized VM provides special APIs requiring substantial OS modifications in user applications

CPU Virtualization

- A CPU architecture is virtualizable if it supports the ability to run the VM's privileged and unprivileged instructions in the CPU's user mode while the VMM runs in supervisor mode.
- Hardware-Assisted CPU Virtualization: This technique attempts to simplify virtualization because full or paravirtualization is complicated

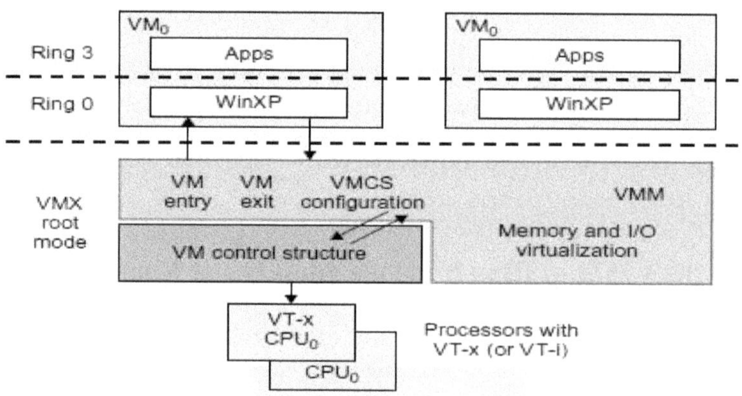

FIGURE 3.11

Intel hardware-assisted CPU virtualization.

(Modified from [68], Courtesy of Lizhong Chen, USC)

Memory Virtualization

- **Memory Virtualization** :the operating system maintains mappings of virtual memory to machine memory using page table
- All modern x86 CPUs include a memory management unit (MMU) and a translation lookaside buffer (TLB) to optimize virtual memory performance
- Two-stage mapping process should be maintained by the guest OS and the VMM, respectively: virtual memory to physical memory and physical memory to machine memory.
- The VMM is responsible for mapping the guest physical memory to the actual machine memory.

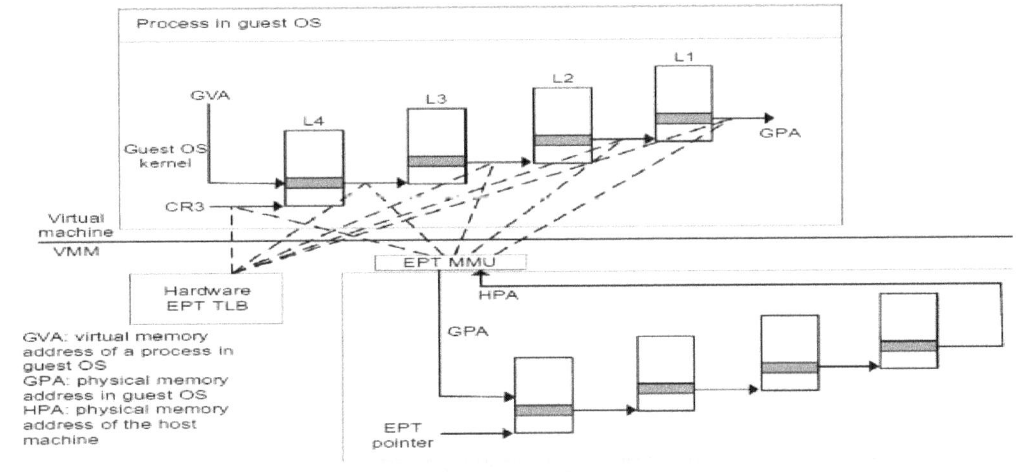

FIGURE 3.13
Memory virtualization using EPT by Intel (the EPT is also known as the shadow page table [68]).

I/O Virtualization

- I/O Virtualization managing the routing of I/O requests between virtual devices and the shared physical hardware
- managing the routing of I/O requests between virtual devices and the shared physical hardware
- Full device emulation emulates well-known, real-world devices All the functions of a device or bus infrastructure, such as device enumeration, identification, interrupts, and DMA, are replicated in software. This software is located in the VMM and acts as a virtual device
- Two-stage mapping process should be maintained by the guest OS and the VMM,

respectively: virtual memory to physical memory and physical memory to machine memory.

- The VMM is responsible for mapping the guest physical memory to the actual machine memory.

Virtualization in Multi-Core Processors

- **Muti-core virtualization** has raised some new **challenges**
- **Two difficulties**: Application programs must be parallelized to use all cores fully, and software must explicitly
- Assign tasks to the cores, which is a very complex problem
- The **first challenge**, new programming models, languages, and libraries are needed to make parallel programming easier.
- The **second challenge** has spawned research involving scheduling algorithms and resource management policies
- **Dynamic heterogeneity** is emerging to mix the fat CPU core and thin GPU cores on the same chip

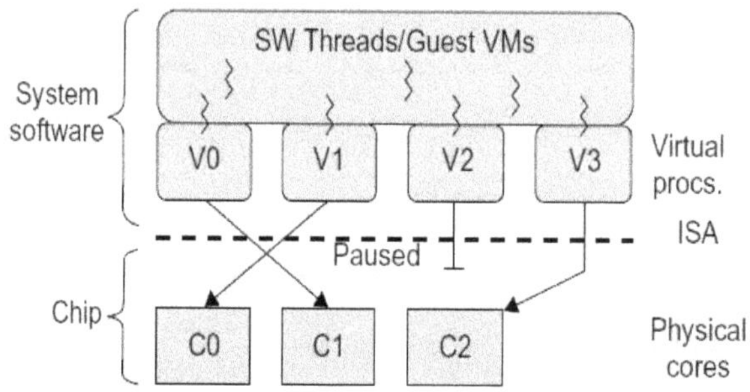

FIGURE 3.16

Multicore virtualization method that exposes four VCPUs to the software, when only three cores are actually present.

(Courtesy of Wells, et al. [74])

- In **many-core chip multiprocessors (CMPs)**→
- Instead of supporting **time-sharing jobs** on one or a few cores, use the abundant cores →**space-sharing**, where single-threaded or multithreaded jobs are simultaneously assigned to separate groups of cores

Physical versus Virtual Clusters

- Virtual clusters are built with VMs installed at distributed servers from one or more physical clusters.
- Assign tasks to the cores, which is a very complex problem
- Fast deployment
- High-Performance Virtual Storage
- reduce duplicated blocks

Virtual Clusters

- **Four ways to manage a virtual cluster**.
- First, you can use a **guest-based manager**, by which the cluster manager resides on a guest system.
- The **host-based manager** supervises the guest systems and can restart the guest system on another physical machine
- Third way to manage a virtual cluster is to use an **independent cluster manager** on both the host and guest systems.
- Finally, use an **integrated cluster** on the guest and host systems.
- This means the manager must be designed to distinguish between virtualized resources and physical resources

Virtualization for data-center automation

- **Data-center automation** means that huge volumes of hardware,software, and database resources in these data centers can be allocated dynamically to millions of Internet users simultaneously, with guaranteed QoS and cost-effectiveness
- This **automation** process is triggered by the growth of virtualization products and cloud computing services.

- The latest virtualization development highlights high availability (HA), backup services, workload balancing, and further increases in client bases.

Server Consolidation in Data Centers

- heterogeneous workloads -chatty workloads and noninteractive workloads
- **Server consolidation** is an approach to improve the low utility ratio of hardware resources by reducing the number of physical servers

Virtual Storage Management

- **storage virtualization** has a different meaning in a system virtualization environment
- **system virtualization,** virtual storage includes the storage managed by VMMs
- and guest OSes data stored in this environment
- can be classified into two categories: VM images and application data.

Cloud OS for Virtualized Data Centers

- Data centers must be virtualized to serve as cloud providers
- **Eucalyptus for Virtual Networking of Private Cloud** :
- Eucalyptus is an **open source software system** intended mainly for supporting **Infrastructure as a Service (IaaS)** clouds
- The system primarily supports **virtual networking** and the management of **VMs**;
- **virtual storage is not supported.**
- Its purpose is to build **private clouds**
- three resource managers
    - Instance Manager
    - Group Manager
    - Cloud Manager

UNIT -3

Introduction to Cloud Computing

- **Cloud computing** allowing **access** to large amounts of **computing power** in a **fully virtualized** manner, by aggregating resources and offering a single system view
- **Cloud computing** has been coined as an umbrella term to describe a category of sophisticated on-demand computing services initially offered by commercial providers, such as Amazon, Google, and Microsoft.
- The main **principle** behind this model is offering computing, storage, and software **"as a service**
- **Cloud** is a parallel and distributed computing system consisting of a collection of **inter-connected and virtualised computers t**hat are dynamically **provisioned**
- The National Institute of Standards and Technology (NIST) characterizes cloud computing as ". . . a pay-per-use model for enabling available, convenient, on-demand network access to a shared pool of configurable computing resources

Common characteristics a cloud should have:

- pay-per-use (no ongoing commitment, utility prices);
- elastic capacity and the illusion of infinite resources;
- self-service interface; and
- resources that are abstracted or virtualised.

ROOTS OF CLOUD COMPUTING

- **Autonomic Computing**: seeks to improve systems by decreasing human involvement in their operation
- **Autonomic, or self-managing**, systems rely on monitoring probes and gauges (sensors), on an adaptation engine (autonomic manager) for computing optimizations based on monitoring data, and on effectors to carry out changes on the system.
- **IBM's Autonomic Computing** Initiative - four properties of autonomic systems: self-configuration, selfoptimization, self-healing, and self-protection.
- **Reference model** for autonomic control loops of **autonomic managers**, called MAPE-K

(Monitor Analyze Plan Execute—Knowledge)

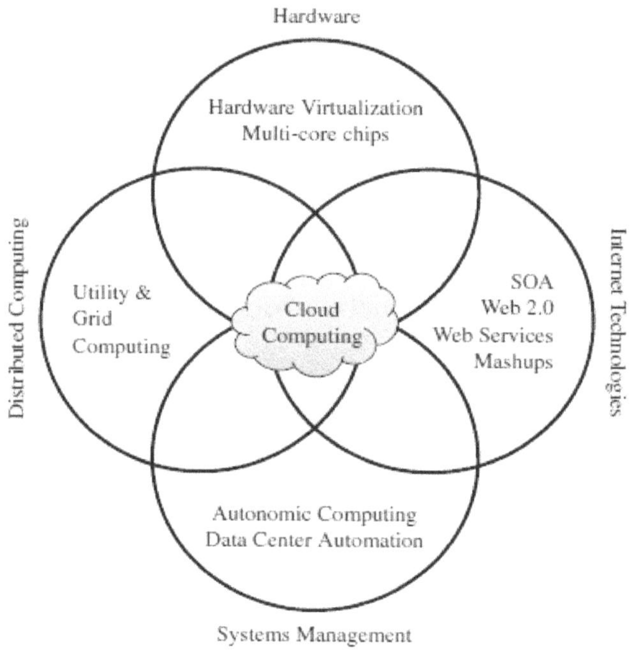

LAYERS AND TYPES OF CLOUDS

- **Cloud computing services** are divided into three classes:
- (1) Infrastructure as a Service,
- (2) Platform as a Service, and
- (3) Software as a Service.
- **Infrastructure as a Service** :A cloud infrastructure enables on-demand provisioning of servers running several choices of operating systems and a customized software stack.
    - **Amazon Web Services** mainly offers IaaS, which in the case of its EC2 service means offering VMs with a software stack that can be customized similar to how an ordinary physical server would be customized.
- **Platform as a Service**: A cloud platform offers an environment on which developers create and deploy applications
    - **Google AppEngine**, an example of Platform as a Service, offers a scalable environment for developing and hosting Web applications

Software as a Service: Traditional desktop applications such as word processing and spreadsheet can now be accessed as a service in the Web. This model of delivering applications, known as Software as a Service (SaaS)

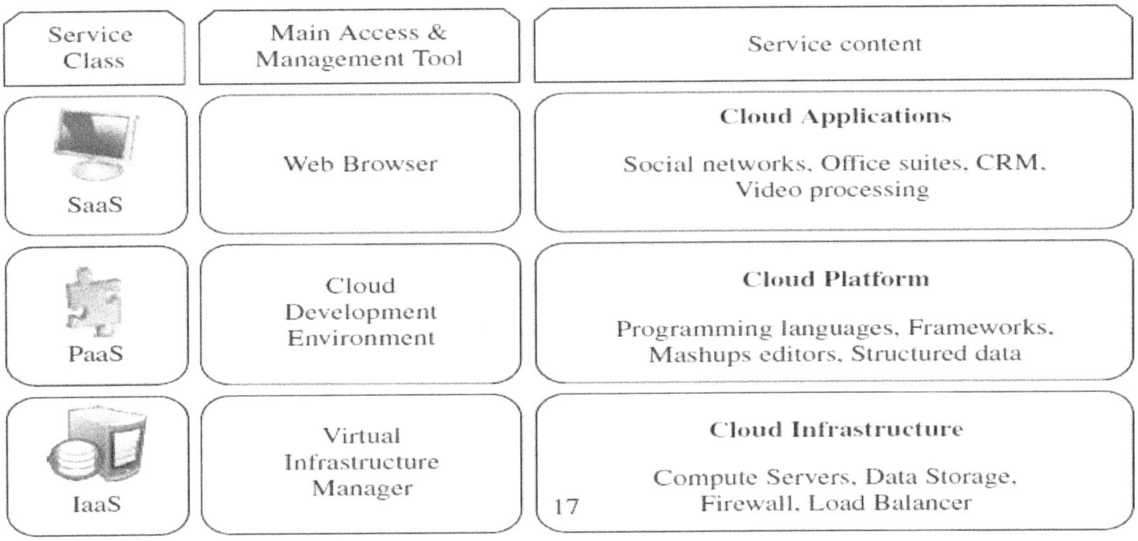

FIGURE 1.3. The cloud computing stack.

Deployment Models

- **Public cloud** as a "cloud made available in a pay-as-you-go manner to the general public" and
- **Private cloud** as "internal data center of a business or other organization, not made available to the general public."
- A **community cloud** is "shared by several organizations and supports a specific community that has shared concerns
- A **hybrid cloud** takes shape when a private cloud is supplemented with computing capacity from public clouds.

- The approach of temporarily renting capacity to handle spikes in load is known as "cloud-bursting"

FIGURE 1.4. Types of clouds based on deployment models.

- **<u>Features of a cloud</u>**
- are **<u>essential</u>** to enable services that truly represent the cloud computing model
- **<u>Self-Service</u>** : clouds must allow self-service access so that customers can request, customize, pay, and use services (expect on-demand, nearly instant access to resources) without intervention of human operators
- **<u>Per-Usage Metering and Billing</u>** : Services must be priced on a shortterm basis (e.g., by the hour), allowing users to release (and not pay for) resources as soon as they are not needed
- **<u>Elasticity</u>** : users expect clouds to rapidly provide resources in any quantity at any time. In particular, it is expected that the additional resources can be
- (a) provisioned, possibly automatically, when an application load increases and
- (b) released when load decreases (scale up and down)

<u>Customization</u>: resources rented from the cloud must be highly customizable.

- In the case of infrastructure services, customization means allowing users to deploy specialized virtual appliances and to be given privileged (root) access to the virtual servers

MIGRATING INTO THE CLOUD

- **Why Migrate?**
- There are economic and business reasons why an enterprise application can be migrated into the cloud, and there are also a number of technological reasons.
- Initiatives in adoption of cloud technologies in the enterprise,
- resulting in integration of enterprise applications running off the captive data centers with the new ones that have been developed on the cloud.

Migration can happen at one of the **five levels** of

- application,
- code,
- design,
- architecture,
- usage

The migration of an enterprise application is best captured by the following

$$P \rightarrow P'_C + P'_l \rightarrow P'_{OFC} + P'_l$$

where

- P is the application before migration running in captive data center,
- P'_C is the application part after migration either into a (hybrid) cloud,
- P'_l is the part of application being run in the captive local data center, and
- P'_{OFC} is the application part optimized for cloud

SEVEN-STEP MODEL OF MIGRATION INTO A CLOUD

FIGURE 2.4. The Seven-Step Model of Migration into the Cloud. (*Source:* Infosys Research.)

Iterative Step

FIGURE 2.5. The iterative Seven-step Model of Migration into the Cloud. (*Source:* Infosys Research.)

Migration Risks and Mitigation

- The biggest challenge to any cloud migration project is how effectively the migration risks are identified and mitigated.
- Migration risks for migrating into the cloud fall under two broad categories:
- the general migration risks
- the security-related migration risks
- several issues identifying all possible production level deviants:
    - the business continuity and disaster recovery in the world of cloud computing service;
    - the compliance with standards and governance issues; the IP and licensing issues;
    - the quality of service (QoS) parameters as well as the corresponding SLAs committed to;
    - the ownership, transfer, and storage of data in the application;
    - the portability and interoperability issues which could help mitigate potential

vendor lock-ins;

On the security front - as addressed in the guideline document published by the Cloud Security Alliance.

- Issues include

- security at various levels of the enterprise application as applicable on the cloud in addition to issues of trust and issues of privacy.
- There are several legal compliances that a migration strategy and implementation has to fulfill,
- including obtaining the right execution logs as well as retaining the rights to all audit trails at a detailed level

Challenges in the Cloud

- Security
- Costing model
- Charging model
- Service level agreement
- Cloud interoperability issue

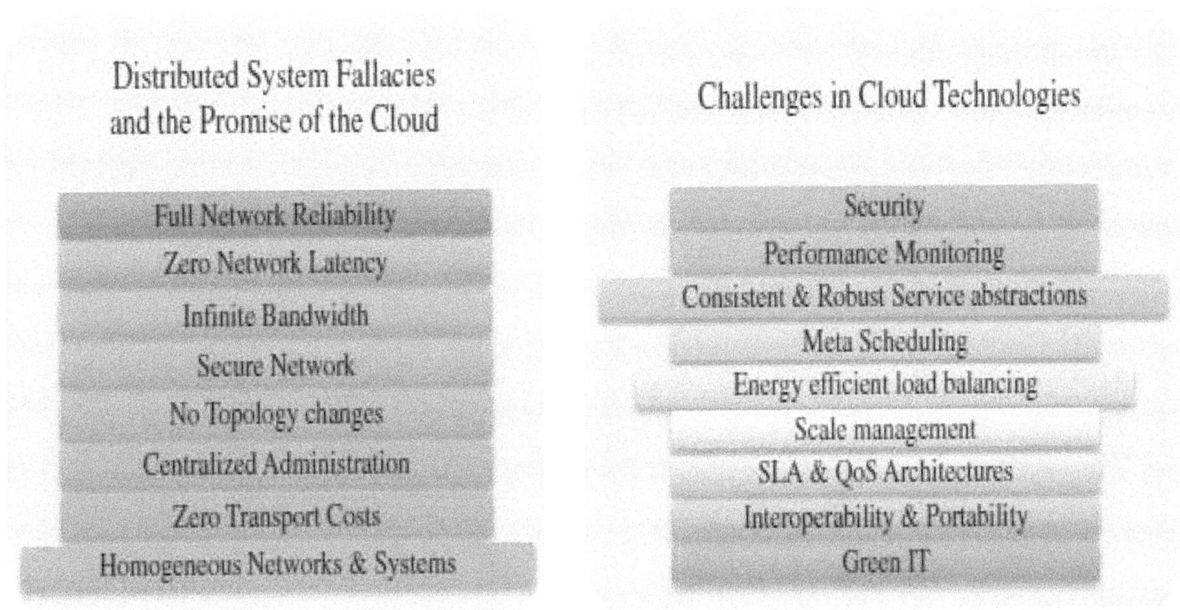

FIGURE 2.3. 'Under the hood' challenges of the cloud computing services implementations.

- Use of cloud computing means dependence on others and that could possibly limit flexibility and innovation:
  - The others are likely become the bigger Internet companies like Google and IBM, who may monopolise the market.
  - Some argue that this use of supercomputers is a return to the time of mainframe computing that the PC was a reaction against.
- Security could prove to be a big issue:
  - It is still unclear how safe out-sourced data is and when using these services ownership of data is not always clear.
- There are also issues relating to policy and access:
  - If your data is stored abroad whose policy do you adhere to?
  - What happens if the remote server goes down?
  - How will you then access files?
  - There have been cases of users being locked out of accounts and losing access to data.

Enterprise cloud computing

Enterprise cloud computing is the alignment of a cloud computing model with an organization's business objectives (profit, return on investment, reduction of operations costs) and processes.

Cloud computing is composed of five essential characteristics:

- on-demand self-service
- broad network access
- resource pooling,
- rapid elasticity
- measured service

The ways in which these characteristics are manifested in an enterprise context vary according to the deployment model employed.

Deployment Models for Enterprise Cloud Computing

- **Public clouds** are provided by a designated service provider for general public under a utility based pay-per-use consumption model. The cloud resources are hosted generally on the service provider's premises
- **Private clouds** are built, operated, and managed by an organization for its internal use only to support its business operations exclusively
- **Virtual private clouds** are a derivative of the private cloud deployment model but are further characterized by an isolated and secure segment of resources, created as an overlay on top of public cloud infrastructure using advanced network virtualization capabilities. Some of the public cloud vendors that offer this capability include Amazon Virtual Private Cloud, OpSource Cloud and Skytap Virtual Lab
- **Community clouds** are shared by several organizations and support a specific community that has shared concerns (e.g., mission, security requirements, policy, and compliance considerations). They

may be managed by the organizations or a third party and may exist on premise or off premise . One example of this is OpenCirrus formed by HP, Intel, Yahoo, and others

- **Managed clouds** arise when the physical infrastructure is owned by and/or physically located in the organization's data centers with an extension of management and security control plane controlled by the managed service provider
- **Hybrid clouds** are a composition of two or more clouds (private, community,or public) that remain unique entities but are bound together by standardized or proprietary technology that enables data and application portability. Some examples of these offerings include Amazon Virtual Private Cloud, Skytap Virtual Lab, and CohesiveF T VPN-Cubed.

Adoption and Consumption Strategies

The selection of strategies for enterprise cloud computing is critical for IT capability as well as for the earnings and costs the organization experiences, motivating efforts toward convergence of business strategies and IT. Critical questions toward this convergence in the enterprise cloud paradigm

- Will an enterprise cloud strategy increase overall business value?
- Are the effort and risks associated with transitioning to an enterprise cloud strategy worth it?
- Which areas of business and IT capability should be considered for the enterprise cloud?
- Which cloud offerings are relevant for the purposes of an organization?
- How can the process of transitioning to an enterprise cloud strategy be piloted and systematically executed?

These questions are addressed from two strategic perspectives:

(1) Adoption (2) Consumption

Adoption strategy : an organization makes a decision to adopt a cloud computing model based on fundamental drivers for cloud computing—scalability, availability, cost and convenience

- **Scalability - Driven Strategy:** The objective is to support increasing workloads of the organization without investment and expenses exceeding returns. The conditions are that the effort, costs (CAPEX and OPEX) and time involved in accessing and installing IT capability on a CDC are less than going through a standard hardware and software procurement and licensing process

- **Availability - Driven Strategy:** Availability has close relations to scalability but is more concerned with the assurance that IT capabilities and functions are accessible, usable and acceptable by the standards of users. This is hence the objective of this basic enterprise cloud strategy.

- **Market-Driven Strategy**: This strategy is more attractive and viable for small, agile organizations tha do not have (or wish to have) massive investments in their IT infrastructure. The objective here is tc identify and acquire the "best deals" for IT capabilities as demand and supply change, enabling ongoing reductions in OPEX and CAPEX.

- **Convenience-Driven Strategy**: The objective is to reduce the load and need for dedicated systen administrators and to make access to IT capabilities by users easier, regardless of their location anc connectivity (e.g. over the Internet). The expectation is that the cost of obtaining IT capabilities from a CDC and making them accessible to users is significantly lower than the cost of having a dedicatec administrator

Consumption Strategy:

The consumption strategies make a distinction between data and application logic because there are questions of programming models used, data sensitivity, software licensing and expected response times that need to be considered.

There are four consumptions strategies identified, where the differences in objectives, conditions and actions reflect the decision of an organization to trade-off hosting costs, controllability and resource elasticity of IT resources for software and data

- **Software Provision**. This strategy is relevant when the elasticity requirement is high for software and low for data, the controllability concerns are low for software and high for data, and the cost reduction concerns for software are high, while cost reduction is not a priority for data, given the high controllability concerns for data, that is, data are highly sensitive

- **Storage Provision**. This strategy is relevant when the elasticity requirements is high for data and low for software, while the controllability of software is more critical than for data. This can be the case for data intensive applications, where the results from processing in the application are more critical and sensitive than the data itself. Furthermore, the cost reduction for data resources is a high concern, hereas cost for software, given its criticality, is not an issue for the organization within reasonable means.
- **Solution Provision**. This strategy is relevant when the elasticity and cost reduction requirements are high for software and data, but the controllability requirements can be entrusted to the CDC. It is not the case that controllability is an insignificant requirement; it is rather the case that the organization trusts the CDC sufficiently to manage access and usage control of its software and data
- **Redundancy Services**. This strategy can be considered as a hybrid enterprise cloud strategy, where the organization switches between traditional, software, storage or solution management based on changes in its operational conditions and business demands

The strategy is referred to as the "redundancy strategy" because the CDC is used for situations such as disaster recovery, fail-over and load balancing

Software, storage or solution services can be implemented using redundancy, such that users are redirected for the purpose of maintaining availability of functionality or performance/response times experienced by the user of the service.

UNIT -4

INFRASTRUCTURE AS A SERVICE PROVIDERS (IAAS)

- Public Infrastructure as a Service providers commonly offer virtual servers containing one or more CPUs, OS, software stack, storage space and communication facilities
- The most relevant features are:
- (i) geographic distribution of data centers;
- (ii) variety of user interfaces and APIs to access the system;
- (iii) specialized components and services that aid particular applications (e.g., loadbalancers,)
- (iv) choice of virtualization platform and operating systems;
- (v) different billing methods and period

Geographic Presence: To improve availability and responsiveness, a provider of worldwide services would typically build several data centers distributed around the world.

- Availability zones are "distinct locations that are engineered to be insulated from failures in other availability zones and provide inexpensive, low-latency network connectivity to other availability zones in the same region."

- **User Interfaces and Access to Servers**.
- Ideally, a public IaaS provider must provide multiple access means to its cloud, thus catering for various usersand their preferences.
- Different types of user interfaces (UI) provide different levels of abstraction, the most common being
  - graphical user interfaces (GUI),
  - command-line tools (CLI), and
  - Web service (WS) APIs.

Advance Reservation of Capacity.

- **Advance reservations** allow users to request for an IaaS provider to reserve resources for a specific time frame in the future, thus ensuring that cloud resources will be available at that time
    - Amazon Reserved Instances is a form of advance reservation of capacity, allowing users to pay a fixed amount of money in advance to guarantee resource availability
- **Automatic Scaling and Load Balancing.**
- As mentioned earlier in this chapter, elasticity is a key characteristic of the cloud computing model.
- Applications often need to scale up and down to meet varying load conditions.
- **Service-Level Agreement**.
- Service-level agreements (SLAs) are offered by IaaS providers to express their commitment to delivery of a certain QoS.
- To customers it serves as a warranty.
    - Amazon EC2 states that "if the annual uptime Percentage for a customer drops below 99.95% for the service year, that customer is eligible to receive a service credit equal to 10% of their bill.3"

- **Hypervisor and Operating System Choice**:
    - Traditionally, IaaS offerings have been based on heavily customized open-source Xen deployments.
    - IaaS providers needed expertise in Linux, networking, virtualization, metering, resource management, and many other low-level aspects to successfully deploy and maintain their cloud offerings.

Public Cloud and Infrastructure Services

- **Public cloud or external cloud**
- describes cloud computing - resources are **dynamically** provisioned via publicly accessible Web applications/Web services (SOAP or RESTful interfaces) from an off-site third-party provider,
- who shares resources and bills on a fine-grained utility computing basis,
- the user pays only for the capacity of the provisioned resources at a particular time

Amazon Elastic Compute Cloud (EC2) is an IaaS service that provides elastic compute capacity in the cloud

Private Cloud and Infrastructure Services

- A **private cloud** aims at providing **public cloud functionality**, but **on private resources**, while maintaining control over an organization's data and resources to meet security and governance's requirements in an organization.
- Private clouds exhibit the following characteristics:
  - Allow service provisioning and compute capability for an organization's users in a self-service manner.
  - Automate and provide well-managed virtualized environments.
  - Optimize computing resources, and servers' utilization.
  - Support specific workloads.
- Examples are Eucalyptus and OpenNebula

"Hybrid cloud"

- in which a combination of private/internal and external cloud resources exist together by enabling outsourcing of noncritical services and functions in public cloud and keeping the critical ones internal
- Release resources from a public cloud and to handle sudden demand usage, which is called "cloud bursting

Cloud and Virtualization Standardization Efforts

- Standardization is important to ensure interoperability between
- virtualization mangement vendors,
- the virtual machines produced by each one of them,
- and cloud computing
- Distributed Management Task Force(DMTF)
- initiated the VMAN (Virtualization Management Initiative),
- delivers broadly supported interoperability and portability standards for managing the virtual computing lifecycle.

OVF (Open Virtualization Format

- VMAN's OVF (Open Virtualization Format) in a collaboration between industry key players: Dell, HP, IBM, Microsoft, XenSource, and Vmware.
- OVF specification provides a common format to package and securely distribute virtual appliances across multiple virtualization platforms.
- VMAN profiles define a consistent way of managing a heterogeneous virtualized environment
- Standardization effort has been initiated by Open Grid Forum (OGF) through organizing an official new working group to deliver a standard API for cloud IaaS, the Open Cloud Computing Interface Working Group (OCCIWG)

VIRTUAL MACHINES PROVISIONING

- Typical life cycle of VM and its major possible states of operation, which make the management and automation of VMs in virtual and cloud environments easier

Process:

- Steps to Provision VM. Here, we describe the common and normal steps of provisioning a virtual server:

- Firstly, you need to select a server from a pool of available servers (physical servers with enough capacity) along with the appropriate OS template you need to provision the virtual machine.
- Secondly, you need to load the appropriate software (operating system you selected in the previous step, device drivers, middleware, and the needed applications for the service required).

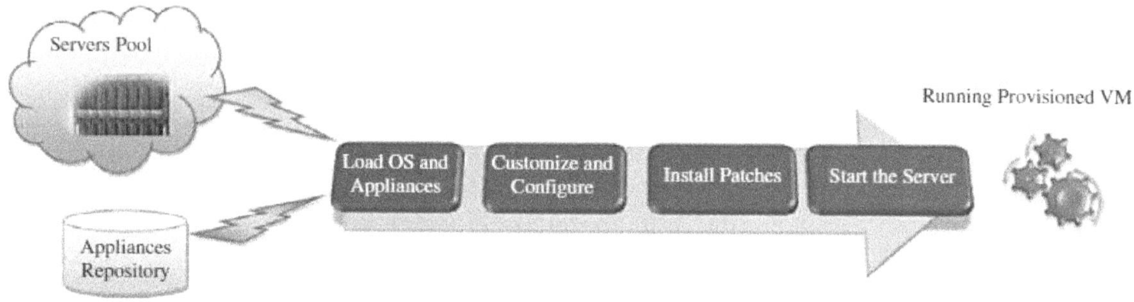

FIGURE 5.4. Virtual machine provision process.

- Thirdly, you need to customize and configure the machine (e.g., IP address, Gateway) to configure an associated network and storage resources.
- Finally, the virtual server is ready to start with its newly loaded software

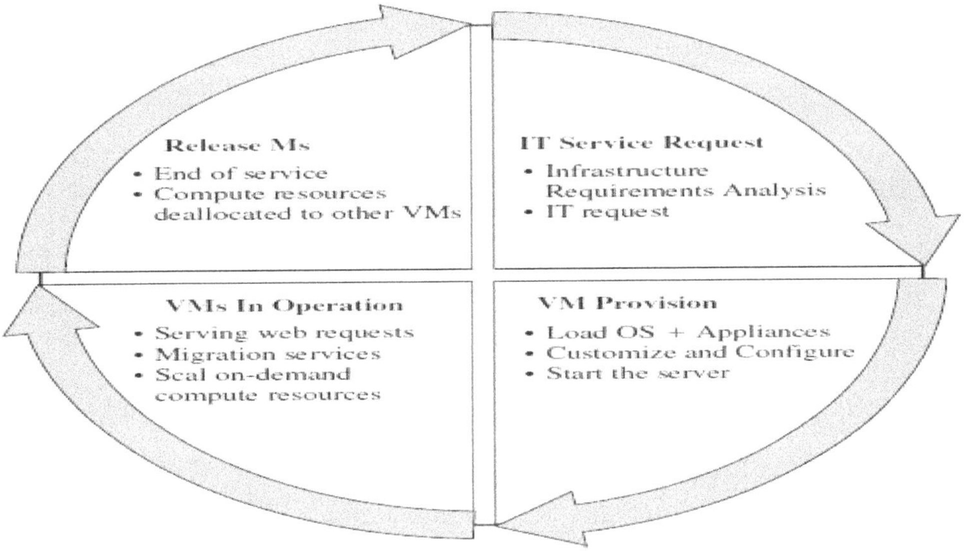

FIGURE 5.3. Virtual machine life cycle.

VIRTUAL MACHINE MIGRATION SERVICES

Migration service,

- in the context of virtual machines, is the process of moving a virtual machine from one host server or storage location to another
- There are different techniques of VM migration,
- hot/life migration,
- cold/regular migration, and
- live storage migration of a virtual machine

VM Migration, SLA and On-Demand Computing:

- virtual machines' migration plays an important role in data centers
- once it has been detected that a particular VM is consuming more than its fair share of resources at the expense of other VMs on the same host,

- it will be eligible, for this machine, to either be moved to another underutilized host or assign more resources for it
- There should be an integration between virtualization's management tools (with its migrations and performance's monitoring capabilities), and SLA's management tools to achieve balance in resources by migrating and monitoring the workloads, and accordingly, meeting the SLA

Migration of Virtual Machines to Alternate Platforms

- Advantages of having facility in data center's technologies is
- to have the **ability to migrate virtual machines** from one platform to another
- For example, the **VMware converter that handles migrations** between ESX hosts;
- the VMware server; and the VMware workstation.
- The VMware converter can also import from other virtualization platforms, such as Microsoft virtual server machines

Deployment Scenario:

- ConVirt deployment consists of at least one ConVirt workstation,
- whereConVirt is installed and ran, which provides the main console for managing the VM life cycle, managing images, provisioning new VMs, monitoring machine resources, and so on.
- There are two essential deployment scenarios for ConVirt:
- A, **basic configuration** in which the Xen or KVM virtualization platform is on the local machine, where ConVirt is already installed; B,
- An **advanced configuration** in which the Xen or KVM is on one or more remote servers.

Installation. The installation process involves the following:

- Installing ConVirt on at least one computer.
- Preparing each managed server to be managed by ConVirt.

- We have two managing servers with the following Ips
- (managed server 1, IP:172.16.2.22; and
- managed server 2, IP:172.16.2.25) as shown in the deployment diagram

Environment, Software, and Hardware. ConVirt 1.1, Linux Ubuntu 8.10, three machines, Dell core 2 due processor, 4G RAM.

- Adding Managed Servers and Provisioning VM.
- Once the installation is done and you are ready to manage your virtual infrastructure, then you can start the ConVirt management console :
- Select any of servers' pools existing (QA Lab in our scenario) and on its context menu, select "Add Server."
- You will be faced with a message asking about the virtualization platform you want to manage (Xen or KVM), as shown in Figure
- Choose KVM, and then enter the managed server information and credentials (IP, username, and password) as shown in Figure
- Once the server is synchronized and authenticated with the management console, it will appear in the left pane/of the ConVirt,

Live Migration Effect on a Running Web Server.

- Clark et al. did evaluate the above migration on an Apache 1.3 Web server; this served static content at a high rate, as illustrated in Figure 5.6.
- The throughput is achieved when continuously serving a single 512-kB file to a set of one hundred concurrent clients.
- This simple example demonstrates that a highly loaded server can be migrated with both controlled impact on live services and a short downtime

VMware Vmotion.

- This allows users to

- (a) automatically optimize and allocate an entire pool of resources for maximum hardware utilization, flexibility, and availability and
- (b) perform hardware's maintenance without scheduled downtime along with migrating virtual machines away from failing or underperforming servers

Citrix XenServerXenMotion.

- This is a nice feature of the Citrix XenServer product, inherited from the Xen live migrate utility, which provides the IT administrator with the facility to move a running VM from one XenServer to another in the same pool without interrupting the service

Regular/Cold Migration.

Cold migration is the migration of a powered-off virtual machine.

- Main **differences between live migration and cold migration** are that
- 1) **live migration needs a shared storage** for virtual machines in the server's pool, but cold migration does not;
- 2) live migration for a virtual machine between two hosts, there would be **certain CPU compatibility checks to be applied**; while in cold migration this checks do not apply
- The cold migration process (VMware) can be summarized as follows:
  - The **configuration files**, including the NVRAM file (BIOS settings), log files, as well as the disks of the virtual machine, are **moved** from the source host to the destination host's associated storage area.
  - The virtual machine is **registered** with the new host.
  - After the migration is completed, the **old version** of the virtual machine is **deleted** from the source host.

Live Storage Migration of Virtual Machine.

- This kind of migration constitutes moving the virtual disks or configuration file of a running virtual machine to a new data store without any interruption in the availability of the virtual machine's service

Aneka

- Manjrasoft Aneka is a .NET-based platform and framework designed for building and deploying distributed applications on clouds.
- It provides a set of APIs for transparently exploiting distributed resources and expressing the business logic of applications by using the preferred programming abstractions.
- Aneka also provides support for deploying and managing clouds.
- By using its Management Studio and a set ofWeb interfaces, it is possible to set up either public or private clouds, monitor their status, update their configuration, and perform the basic management operations.

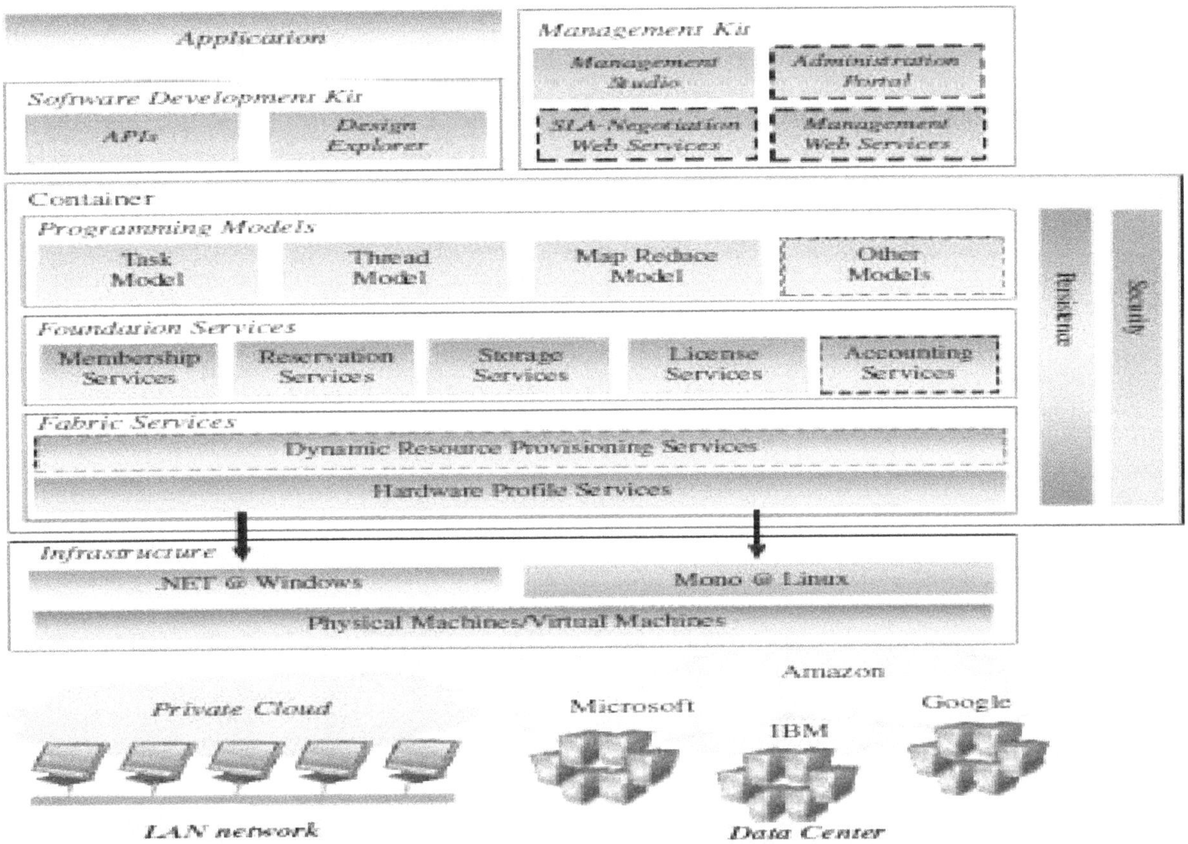

FIGURE 5.22. Manjrasoft Aneka layered architecture [10].

UNIT-5

SAAS

- SaaS is a model of software deployment where an application is hosted as a service provided to customers across the Internet.
- Saas alleviates the burden of software maintenance/support but users relinquish control over software versions and requirements

SaaS Maturity Model

Level 1: Ad-Hoc/Custom – One Instance per customer

Level 2: Configurable per customer

Level 3: configurable & Multi-Tenant-Efficient

Level 4: Scalable, Configurable & Multi-Tenant-Efficient

SaaS INTEGRATION PRODUCTS AND PLATFORMS

- Cloud-centric integration solutions are being developed and demonstrated for showcasing their capabilities for integrating enterprise and cloud applications.
- Composition and collaboration will become critical and crucial for the mass adoption of clouds

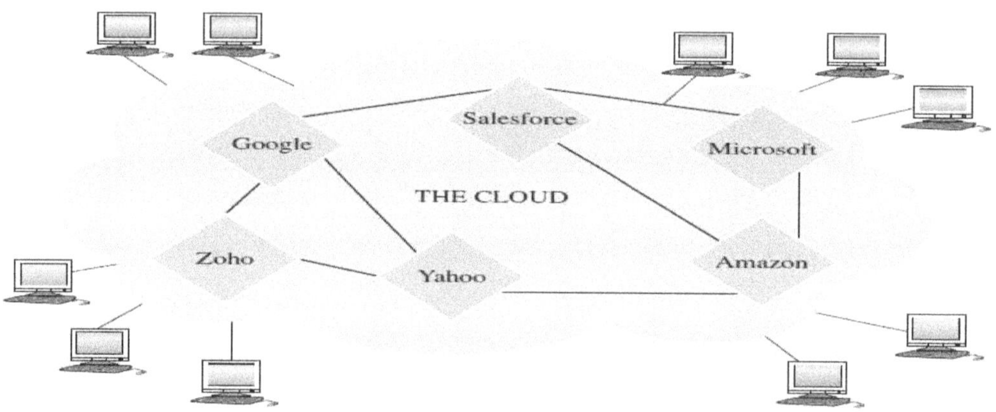

FIGURE 3.4. The Smooth and Spontaneous Cloud Interaction via Open Clouds.

Jitterbit:

- Jitterbit is a fully graphical integration solution that provides users a versatile platform
- suite of productivity tools to reduce the integration efforts sharply.
- Jitterbit can be used standalone or with existing EAI infrastructures
- Help us quickly design, implement, test, deploy, and manage the integration projects

  Two major components :
- Jitterbit Integration Environment
- An intuitive point-and-click graphical UI that enables to quickly configure, test, deploy and manage integration projects on the Jitterbit server.
- Jitterbit Integration Server
- A powerful and scalable run-time engine that processes all the integration operations, fully configurable and manageable from the Jitterbit application.

Linkage with On premise and on demand Applications

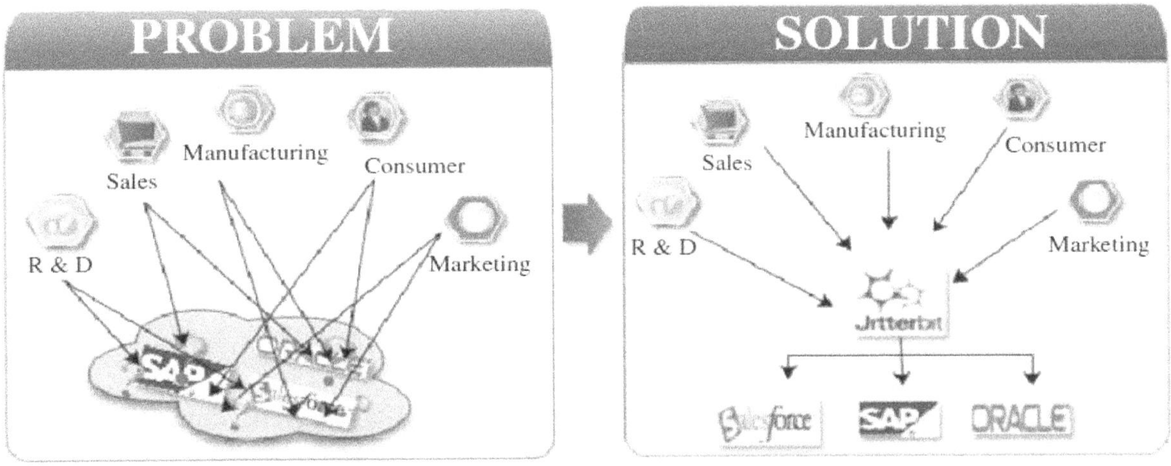

FIGURE 3.5. Linkage of On-Premise with Online and On-Demand Applications.

Google APP Engine

- The app engine is a Cloud-based platform, is quite comprehensive and combines infrastructure as a service (IaaS), platform as a service (PaaS) and software as a service (SaaS).

- The app engine supports the delivery, testing and development of software on demand in a Cloud computing environment that supports millions of users and is highly scalable.
- The company extends its platform and infrastructure to the Cloud through its app engine. It presents the platform to those who want to develop SaaS solutions at competitive costs.

Google is a leader in web-based applications,

so it's not surprising that the company also offers cloud development services.

- These services come in the form of the Google App Engine, which enables developers to build their own web applications utilizing the same infrastructure that powers Google's powerful applications.
- The Google App Engine provides a fully integrated application environment. Using Google's development tools and computing cloud, App Engine applications are easy to build, easy to maintain, and easy to scale. All you have to do

Features of App Engine

- These are covered by the depreciation policy and the service-level agreement of the app engine. Any changes made to such a feature are backward-compatible and implementation of such a feature is usually stable. These include data storage, retrieval, and search; communications; process management; computation; app configuration and management.

- Data storage, retrieval, and search include features such as HRD migration tool, Google Cloud SQL, logs, datastore, dedicated Memcache, blobstore, Memcache and search.
- Communications include features such as XMPP. channel, URL fetch, mail, and Google Cloud Endpoints.
- Process management includes features like scheduled tasks and task queue
- Computation includes images.

- App management and configuration cover app identity, users, capabilities, traffic splitting, modules, SSL for custom domains, modules, remote access, and multitenancy

Centralizing email Communications

- The key here is to enable anywhere/anytime access to email.
- Precloud computing, your email access was via a single computer, which also stored all your email messages. For this purpose, you probably used a program like Microsoft Outlook or Outlook Express, installed on your home computer.
- To check your home email from work, it took a bit of juggling and perhaps the use of your ISP's email access web page. That web page was never in sync with the messages on your home PC, of course, which is just the start of the problems with trying to communicate in this fashion.
- A better approach is to use a web-based email service, such as Google's Gmail (mail.google.com), Microsoft's Windows Live Hotmail (mail.live.com), or Yahoo! Mail (mail.yahoo.com). These services place your email inbox in the cloud; you can access it from any computer connected to the Internet.

Collaborating via Web-Based Communication Tools

GMAIL

- Gmail offers a few unique features that set it apart from the web-based email crowd.
- First, Gmail doesn't use folders. With Gmail you can't organize your mail into folders, as you can with the other services.
- Instead, Gmail pushes the search paradigm as the way to find the messages you want—not a surprise, given Google's search-centric business model.
- Gmail does, however, let you "tag" each message with one or more labels. This has the effect of creating virtual folders, as you can search and sort your messages by any of their labels.
- In addition, Gmail groups together related email messages in what Google calls conversations

www.ingramcontent.com/pod-product-compliance
Ingram Content Group UK Ltd.
Pitfield, Milton Keynes, MK11 3LW, UK
UKHW061540190726
13845UKWH00031B/1137

9 789349 922198